Praise for

The Power of Attention

"*The Power of Attention* is a journey into the nature of awareness that reveals how your simple focus not only enlivens your being but also leads to the fulfillment of your innermost desires."

— **Deepak Chopra**, author of *You Are the Universe*

"What we focus on expands! *The Power of Attention* is an invaluable guide for anyone seeking to regain the power of attention and discover its source: the vibration of universal love that is our natural state of being."

— **James Van Praagh**, spiritual medium and
author of *The Power of Love*

"Meditation is one of the great joys of my life.
Sarah McLean's teachings, her story, and her humor really left an impression on me. Even the energy in her meditation studio in Sedona was powerful. This book is a great way to tap into her wealth of knowledge to gain support on your journey to awakening to love."

— **India Arie**, Grammy Award–winning
singer, songwriter, songversationalist

"This book offers brilliant guidance on cultivating the power of your attention through meditation and mindfulness training. **Sarah McLean** masterfully imparts essential wisdom that will transform your perspective on life, love, and fulfillment."

— **Marci Shimoff**, #1 *New York Times* best-selling
author of *Happy for No Reason*

"If you want to become radically alive, harness the power of your mind. **Sarah McLean** is a true teacher who will show you how. She's trekked the world, studied with masters, read the science, and spent decades personally experiencing her own greatest love within through meditation. Now she puts this grounded, easy-to-apply, vital wisdom at our fingertips. Get ready for infinite love."

— **Tama Kieves**, *USA Today*–featured visionary career coach and author of *Inspired & Unstoppable* and *A Year Without Fear*

"**Sarah McLean** lifts lessons from her decades of work with meditation; filters them through real-life experience; and offers us a surprisingly practical, reliable guide to growth. Her message that we must learn to pay attention is striking and right on. This is not the work of an idle self-help dreamer; it is the harvest of a life of spiritual insight. To know Sarah is to know love: deep, profound, unquestioned love. In *The Power of Attention*, she puts that love within reach of every reader."

— **Mary Fisher**, political activist, artist, and author of *Messenger*

"*The Power of Attenton* is a treasure-filled discourse on how to regain the power of attention and how to discover its source: the powerful field of loving awareness that lives through you as you. It's a beautifully written, insightful, and inspiring read."

— **Colette Baron-Reid**, intuition expert, spiritual medium, and author of *Uncharted*

ALSO BY SARAH MCLEAN

Books

Soul-Centered: Transform Your Life in 8 Weeks with Meditation*

CDs

Guidance for a Soul-Centered Life: An 8 Week Program (5-CD set)

Meditate: Guided Meditations with Sarah McLean

What Is Soul-Centeredness? (2-CD set)

*Available from Hay House

Please visit:

Hay House USA: www.hayhouse.com®
Hay House Australia: www.hayhouse.com.au
Hay House UK: www.hayhouse.co.uk
Hay House South Africa: www.hayhouse.co.za
Hay House India: www.hayhouse.co.in

The Power of Attention

Awaken to Love and Its Unlimited Potential with Meditation

Sarah McLean

HAY HOUSE, INC.

Carlsbad, California • New York City
London • Sydney • Johannesburg
Vancouver • New Delhi

Published and distributed in the United States by: Hay House, Inc.: www.hay house.com® • *Published and distributed in Australia by:* Hay House Australia Pty. Ltd.: www.hayhouse.com.au • *Published and distributed in the United Kingdom by:* Hay House UK, Ltd.: www.hayhouse.co.uk • *Published and distributed in the Republic of South Africa by:* Hay House SA (Pty), Ltd.: www.hayhouse.co.za • *Distributed in Canada by:* Raincoast Books: www.raincoast.com • *Published in India by:* Hay House Publishers India: www.hayhouse.co.in

Cover design: Amy Grigoriou • *Interior design:* Pamela Homan

Library of Congress Cataloging-in-Publication Data

Names: McLean, Sarah, date, author.
Title: The power of attention : awaken to love and its unlimited potential
    with meditation / Sarah McLean.
Description: Carlsbad : Hay House, Inc., 2017.
Identifiers: LCCN 2016037603 | ISBN 9781401942250 (paperback)
Subjects: LCSH: Attention. | Self-consciousness (Awareness) | Meditation. |
    BISAC: SELF-HELP / Meditations. | BODY, MIND & SPIRIT / Meditation.
Classification: LCC BF321 .M35 2017 | DDC 153.7/33--dc23 LC record available at
https://lccn.loc.gov/2016037603

ISBN: 978-1-4019-4225-0

10 9 8 7 6 5 4 3 2 1
1st edition, February 2017

Printed in the United States of America

To you, the
embodiment
of love

CONTENTS

INTRODUCTION

Your attention is a superpower. It has the power to change your world. Not only does your attention have a powerful effect on the people and things that you focus it on, it also has the power to connect you with everything else in creation. When you become the master of your attention and use it purposefully, you can transform your life, inside and out.

How do you feel when you are being seen, being heard, being *paid attention to*, without condition or obligation? Whether it's the undivided, gentle attention of a lover, a parent, a child, a dear friend, or even your pet, what you probably feel is connected and loved. Your natural attention has that effect, too.

Consider this: your bare attention is a currency. After all, you *pay* attention, and when you do, this currency connects you to and has a very real impact on whatever or whomever you focus it on. Your attention has the power to enliven and nourish all that you attend to. Your attention is the currency of love.

This book is about reclaiming the power of your attention. We'll look at how you use it, how you unwittingly give it away, and how you can harness it to experience more love in your life.

You'll build your attention muscle through the training of meditation and mindfulness so you can more easily focus on what you want when you want, without distraction. You'll also learn techniques to access the unlimited potential of the source of your attention: love itself.

Seek and You Will Find

You may be familiar with the phrase, "What you seek, you shall find." In my experience, this is true. Your attention, the intention that accompanies it, and where you focus it can alter your perception of reality.

Just as shining a flashlight into a darkened room brings to light whatever the beam is cast upon, your attention lights up whatever you pay attention to. Attention can also bring to light what you are seeking or have the desire to know.

When you are consciously on a quest, your attention and intentions call responses into being—be they creative inspirations, kindness, beauty, greater health and vitality, purposeful work, fulfilling relationships, answers to questions, or even signs or synchronicities pointing you in the right direction. In other words, what you are seeking, or your way to it, will be illuminated simply by the act of seeking! Your attention is that powerful, because the source of your attention is so powerful. It has the power to bring *everything* into being.

We all want to feel more deeply engaged with the world around us, with those we love, and with the passion and purpose that make life worth living. Yet many of us will spend the majority of our lives searching for those feelings of love and fulfillment outside of ourselves, in people, conditions, material objects, or sensory experiences. The ultimate irony, of course, is that what we are looking for has been within each one of us all along. We often make this inner discovery only after we've traveled far and wide in our search. I know this from personal experience.

A Quest

I've been on a quest since I was very young. I was curious and wanted to *know*. I love mysteries. I read every single detective story and savored books about mystics, alchemy, earth energies, spontaneous healing, and the soul. Before I was old enough to understand why, I was on a quest to connect to something deeper.

I wasn't a peaceful child. I was often anxious and in tears both at home and at school. Though I was sociable, deep inside I felt like a bad girl. Now I understand that I was dealing with the stress of a turbulent, sometimes violent home environment.

At 17, I lived up to my bad-girl persona and checked out emotionally and physically. I dropped out of high school and left home, eventually living homeless on a beach in South Florida. Almost a year passed before I decided to join the military. During basic training, I eloped with a man that I had been living with on the beach. He was violent toward me, and after a year, I'd had enough and got a divorce. I got my GED and headed off to college.

By the time I was 24, I was sharing a triple-decker with other twentysomethings in Cambridge, Massachusetts. I was bartending at a restaurant in Copley Square while I finished up my degree. I became friends with Tom, one of my housemates. He worked as a room-service waiter at a local hotel. We'd both come home after midnight from work and watch foreign films together. He loved to write and paint. Starry-eyed and full of dreams, we fell in love.

He wanted to travel the world, and I wanted to go with him. We planned a two-year trip to explore what we could of the world by mountain bike. We would begin in Europe and then travel into Asia and beyond. We saved money to buy equipment and to travel with, and in June we were ready to go. I imagined that we were going on a quest to discover the secrets of this life.

We landed in Athens and it was already a very hot summer. This was a time before cell phones and handheld navigation systems. We navigated the Greek language and the road signs relying on a pocket English/Greek dictionary, a few maps, and a compass. Our bikes were fully loaded with gear to last many months and seasons on the road: a tent, sleeping bags, a gas stove, a bicycle pump, tire patches, toiletries, four changes of clothing each, and lots of wool socks for the cooler months.

We explored ancient ruins in the land of mythology and Orphism, gods and goddesses, and mathematics and drama. We visited the Acropolis, temples, and massive ancient theaters. We journeyed through the wild, rugged regions of the Peloponnese and the Mani Peninsula and its southernmost tip known as the "Gate of Hell."

According to climate records, it was Greece's hottest summer. I truly wasn't able to cycle for more than 10 minutes at a time because of the searing-hot sun. I'd have to rest along the shadeless roadside, seriously contemplating whether to throw my bike from the top of each of the hills we climbed. Tom would talk me out of it. He was half-Greek and physically handled it much better than I.

I sweated and pedaled my way through the desolate wasteland. I was in hell, and had no doubt that this land's earlier occupants had felt the same way.

Though spectacular, it was a grim and barren place. Stone towers dotted the landscape, each with its own cemetery. Generations of families had lived in these now abandoned towers. The story goes that when someone was insulted or offended, they'd get their entire family to engage in a bloody vendetta against the offender's family, and the towers were their means of defense. Apparently, they made good refuges from the assailants. As the hours and days wore on, I developed a theory about why these people were so aggressive: it was the heat.

It was in Mani that my anxiety was getting the best of me. And we'd only been gone a few weeks. I was concerned this trip wasn't for me. That's when Tom introduced me to a simple Buddhist chant he had learned at the Zen center in Cambridge where he used to meditate.

I wrote down each line of the chant and slid it into the plastic sleeve atop the maps in my handlebar pack. As I road, I'd read it and chant silently. Chanting helped to keep my attention on the present moment, so when I looked at the hills ahead that I'd soon have to climb, I would focus on my chant instead of my self-defeating thoughts. Chanting also helped me to keep up my cadence, much like when we'd used the call-and-response songs while we marched in basic training. ("I had a good home and I left," "*Your right!*")

I hadn't realized that this chant, *Enmei Jukku Kannon Gyo*, is a Japanese chant to appeal to Kanzeon, known elsewhere as Quan Yin, the Chinese Goddess of Mercy, the One Who Sees and Hears the Cry from the Human World. I chanted for hours on end, every day for months. It worked. I was able to pay attention to the silent sound of the chant rather than to the ongoing discouraging thoughts in my own mind. Little did I know that I was experiencing the profound effects of chanting and mantra and learning an important lesson about attention.

A month later, we biked into Istanbul, Turkey—once known as Constantinople—and toured the great mosques. Outside the great structures, I had to defend myself when young men groped me. They thought Western women, especially blondes like me, were into it. Apparently, they had seen too many European pornographic magazines featuring blond women. I wasn't afraid, but I was bothered by it. I learned the words for sister (*kardes*) and mother (*anne*) and did my best to form a sentence that I hoped meant, "You wouldn't do that to your mother or sister."

Then we headed north to the Black Sea to explore more ancient churches, castles, and monasteries, these towering above the wild coastline. We slept on the ground under the stars in that land of great philosophers and those who revered the cycles of nature. It was very windy, and more than once my chant was hijacked by the words of Bob Seger's "Against the Wind."

As we headed into the interior of Turkey, we learned about the Sufi whirling dervishes and their hidden mystic traditions that thrived in the middle of the country. Whirling is a devotional ceremonial dance that symbolizes letting go of the ego and creating a one-pointed focus on God.

We traveled into the Cappadocia region, with its striking volcanic terrain marked by thousands of towering rock spires, called fairy chimneys. It was a land of refuge centuries ago, where monks and mystics carved their homes and churches into rock columns. They developed underground cities with tunnels and chambers to protect themselves and practice their religious beliefs in safety.

We made it to Pakistan as the chill of autumn set in. Because it was not acceptable for a woman to travel into villages, never mind by bike, I cropped my hair and dressed as a young man. In disguise, I could enter and eat a meal in the tea shops along the way. We cycled uphill for days along the Silk Route in the foothills of the Himalayas.

We passed a long line of trucks and buses that had been stuck on the route literally for days blocked by enormous rockslides brought on by the rainy season. The rocks were being cleared manually by local men, but it was certainly slow going. We were able to continue on the road as we carried our bikes over the huge boulders and rocks. Sometimes we'd scale down the hillsides carrying the bikes to the banks of the Indus River, then climb up again to get around the impasse.

There was something deeply compelling about the powerful, dramatic landscape. This area was the birthplace of the Vedas, the 5,000-year-old wisdom tradition of yogis and mystics, which I would study years later. This was the place where I felt most content. The terrain was rugged. We were mostly alone, as it was sparsely inhabited, and there was very little activity on the road.

We cycled north into the Swat Valley, where the Karakoram and Hindu Kush mountain ranges meet. It's called the Switzerland of the East, and with its lakes and hills and lushness, it is one of the most beautiful places in the world. Centuries ago, it was the home of Hinayana, Tantric, and Mahayana Buddhism, with over 1,400 monasteries. At the time I was visiting, it was becoming the home of fundamentalist Islam. By 2007, it would come under the control of the Taliban.

As we biked, we began seeing solitary men every few hundred feet in the hills, each seeming to appear out of nowhere. Each stood still, watching us intently as if on guard, wrapped in a dark wool blanket, equipped with a long rifle, and carrying the flag that identified the tribe he belonged to. Though I was still dressed like a male, with my woolen vest, scarf, and hat, I doubted I was getting away with my disguise.

As dusk settled in, we were still 20 kilometers from the only place to stay in the area, and, for the first time on the trip, I was frightened. I felt the cold stares of men lurking in the landscape, silently stalking us as we steadily pedaled along. Then in the distance, we heard the rumble of a truck; soon, a Swiss Red Cross truck rattled by. They were heading to their makeshift headquarters, an office in the old palace of the king of Swat where we were going to be staying. I hoped they noted that we, too, were going in their direction.

We arrived at our destination safely and were the only guests there. We were assigned a large room in the palace. Remnants of luxury were now moldy and ramshackle. By the light of the candle, two tarantulas that called the room home cast large, unmoving shadows on the wall. I was so exhausted from the exertion and fear I'd just experienced that I slept soundly even in their company.

We awoke the next morning and continued north on the icy road, climbing to an altitude of over 8,000 feet toward the Chinese border. We stopped in the mountainous Hunza Valley, a place worthy of being called heaven on earth with its glorious landscape. The snowcapped peaks were the backdrop to the terraced hillsides, cultivated with crops as far as we could see. Apricot, apple, and other fruit trees were plentiful, and there seemed to be joy in the air.

The inhabitants are said to have extraordinarily long, disease-free lives. They believe that goat's leg soup and the almond-flavored kernels found inside apricot pits hold the secret to longevity. Here, women were held in equal esteem as men and appeared to run the town, working as shopkeepers, farmers, and managers of guesthouses. What a difference in culture!

After a few days we learned from the locals that the pass into China was unpassable and closed due to snow, so we headed south. We could not make it into India as planned due to skirmishes and an unsafe situation in the Punjab. That's when we flew from Islamabad into Thailand. We wanted to get warm.

In Bangkok, I was amazed by the many huge, gold-hued Buddha shrines where people would offer fruits, money, and prayers before setting off to shop in the multistoried malls found everywhere in this city. I was astounded by this seamless and casual relationship between religion and materialism, consciousness and commerce.

We made our way to a little island just south of Bangkok where we stayed in a little grass hut and relaxed for a week by the sea. We then biked north to Chiang Mai. Tom wasn't feeling well, so he stayed at the guesthouse while I joined a group who were trekking into the Golden Triangle. These were lands inhabited by the hill tribes, who weren't actual tribes per se, but highlanders who lived off the grid as farmers. It's called the triangle because that's where Thailand, Laos, and Burma converge; and it's an area only accessible by foot.

As we'd trek into small enclaves of simple wooden houses with tin roofs, mothers wearing distinctive headdresses adorned with coins, beads, and shells, followed by their shiny-faced children, came out to greet us, happy to sell us their crafts. Though they dressed ornately, they lived simply as farmers who hadn't yet given up their deep connection with nature and her rhythms.

When I returned from the trek three days later, Tom was delirious and had a really high fever. I ran to flag down a rickshaw to take him to the only hospital in the area. He spent a week there being treated for pneumonia. When he was released, we decided to return home.

I returned to the States with a global perspective. Nine months of sleeping on the ground, being outside, exploring various terrains and cultures, and confronting my fears and physical limitations brought me closer to the natural world and to my own nature. I saw the light in every person's eyes, repeatedly falling in love with strangers who quickly became dear friends I'd never see again.

Though I'd traveled thousands of miles, I hadn't unlocked the mysteries of life. I don't know what I had expected from this trip, really—perhaps a journey to the center of my soul.

It's All Right Here

Once we were back home, Tom and I went our separate ways. He pursued a master's degree at an art school and I moved to Washington, D.C., to work for a family friend who had a real-estate development company. It didn't take long before I was successful by worldly standards: I bought a late-model car complete with a giant car phone (it was 1988). I became a co-owner of a four-story brownstone, and I had plenty of money in the bank.

Although I had attained what seemed to make others happy—a house, a car, a good paying job—I didn't feel content. Instead, I was restless. I still longed for something I couldn't quite put my finger on. Maybe it was peace or love, or maybe it was a desire to know God. So my quest continued.

It was only months later that I met a radiant young man who was really into meditation. He'd grown up in a family that had been meditating together since he was a child. He suggested that meditation might be something that would make me happier, and I believed him. One Sunday afternoon in a small upstairs room of a brownstone in Dupont Circle, I learned to meditate. (I share this story in Chapter 3.)

I will never forget that day; it was then that I found what I had been searching for in those far-off places, and I didn't even have to leave the country. With my eyes closed in meditation, I felt the most profound peace and connection. I felt as if I had found my real home, and it was inside of me. It is a place of deep silence, comfort, and love.

I have practiced meditation ever since that day. It has continued to take me on an internal journey which, so far, has transformed every area of my life and how I see the world and myself. Meditation has connected me to the deepest source of all that exists, and this has helped me feel more connected to myself and more intimate with everything and everyone that surrounds me.

Knowing the Place

I have always loved a verse from T. S. Eliot's "Little Gidding." After practicing meditation for a while, I understood it through new eyes:

> And the end of all our exploring
> Will be to arrive where we started
> And know the place for the first time.

Meditation had given me a glimpse of "the place" that Eliot was speaking of. It's the birthplace of everyone and everything, though it's not a physical location: it's a field of potential. It's that consciousness that underlies all condition, form, and creation. Physicists say that everything in creation emerges from this indivisible field of awareness. Yogis and mystics must know this, too. *This* is our true home.

This field expresses itself through each and every one of us *as us*. It's the source of your attention and mine. It's that consciousness that is looking through your eyes.

You too can become intimate with this vast inner world through the practice of meditation. Meditation allows your nervous system to settle down so you can transcend your five senses and dive into this field. It is a subtle realm, without dimension. It surrounds you and binds your atoms together. It binds the entire universe together. It is the field of love.

This field of pure love and awareness has been with me all along, in the same way that it has always been with you. In fact, it *is* you. With this new realization, you'll see everything and everyone as if you are seeing them for the very first time—as an expression of love.

The Currency of Your Attention

Through the pages of this book, you'll learn to look at attention in a whole new way. When you do, you'll honor it and recognize the value of this precious currency that is inherent in you and in everyone else.

You'll learn mindfulness and meditation practices that will help you train your attention so you can be more in charge of how and where you focus it. These practices will also reveal to you the limits that veil your ability to give your attention, and the barriers you have erected between you and that which wants to give you attention. Once they are revealed, you can begin to dismantle them.

Once your attention is unmasked, you'll meet each moment and each endeavor with greater presence, curiosity, and love. With your greater ability to be present, you'll be attentive to the signs and wonders that will point your way to your very best life. Whether it's a call to express a passion, pursue a talent, or share your gifts, each will show you the way to your full potential.

You'll also learn how to connect to that peaceful center within—a center that you'll know as home, and one that you can return to anytime, whether in or out of meditation. This center is the source of your attention, and by paying attention to it, you'll tap into its organizing power, wisdom, and evolutionary capability.

I hope this book serves as a guide to reclaim your attention, improve your ability to sustain it, and help you awaken to the love that is its source.

Chapter 1

Matters of Attention

To pay attention, this is our endless and proper work.

—MARY OLIVER

Three decades ago I was being trained to pay attention. I was in basic training in the U.S. Army, and when a superior would call us to *attention*, I'd stop what I was doing—whether polishing my boots or walking to the mess hall—and in an instant, straighten up, stand with my heels together, toes apart, chin up, chest out, shoulders back, and stomach in. My arms would shoot stiffly down by my sides and, with my fingers straightened, my middle fingers would line up precisely with the seams of my fatigues. I'd assume a blank expression, eyes forward and focused on some random distant object, and wait, motionless until the next command—which I hoped would be, "As you were," so I could get back to the task at hand.

Now, and for the past two decades, I've been teaching people how to pay attention through the practice of meditation and mindfulness. Most meditations don't ask you to stare blankly at some random distant point. Instead, you are to choose a focus and bring your gentle attention to it, whether it is an internal sound such as a silently repeated mantra, an external visual focus such as a candle flame, or the sensation of breath moving in and out of your body.

As you meditate, like in life, your attention will likely drift, and when you realize it, you redirect your attention to the focus, again and again. This is the gist of the *practice* of meditation—the training of one's attention. This training not only develops your ability to be more attentive while in meditation but also makes you more attentive outside of meditation so you can live a more deliberate, aware, and meaningful life.

Your attention is a natural resource—an invaluable currency that you spend every single day. You couldn't really function without it. The kind of attention I am referring to here is your nonjudgmental, natural attention. It's what you are using to read these words. This attention arises from somewhere inside you. It's the unseen, subtle, powerful vehicle that enables you to connect and engage with the world. It is what forges relationships with the objects of your attention. It's also the key to success in relationships, work, creativity, and pleasure.

Your attention is powerful. It energizes and enlivens what you focus it on. Scientists have proven this. Your loved ones feel it, your co-workers recognize it, and, if you reflect on the various arenas of your life, you'll quickly realize it, too. What you pay attention to, you encourage to thrive. For this reason, what you pay attention to and how you pay attention are of extreme importance.

You Scored

Attention is so powerful that nearly every form of life devotes a significant amount of energy to attaining it from the world around them. It's natural to need it: babies cry for it, pets beg for it, your body demands it, and flowers bloom for it. No matter what source it is sought from, all beings depend on some kind of attention to survive and to thrive.

Chances are you've already been blessed with a great amount of being attended to. I know I have. Most of us were born into families that cared for, fed, clothed, and sheltered us, and made our well-being their priority. We had teachers and friends who paid attention to us in school. As adults we have co-workers, neighbors, family, and friends who care about us. When you really pay attention, you'll find that almost everywhere you look, there are people who see us, recognize us, listen to us, and give their attention to us, whether we know them or not.

Perhaps you have never considered how supported you are, just by virtue of being right here, alive, in this moment, on this Earth. There's the bounty of natural resources that sustains your life, including the plant and animal kingdoms whose lives you depend on for nourishment, and even the bees who pollinate the trees for your fruit and nuts.

You are also supported by many, many people's efforts: those who attend to and carefully make your clothes and those who design and manufacture the machines you use, the furniture you sit on, and the home you live in. There are those who sow the seeds, those who tend the plants, and those who pick and ship the produce you eat. There are those who service your needs at home and at work. When you really pay attention, you will discover that there is support everywhere.

Paying Attention

Your attention is a limited resource. You don't have enough of it to pay attention to everything all the time, so you have to choose what you want to pay attention to, and your brain also chooses for you by filtering out irrelevant items. Your total attentional capacity is called your *vigilant attention*. That capacity varies from person to person, from moment to moment, and is affected to various degrees by fatigue, boredom, aging, and interest.

Your attention is allocated based on the need, task, or situation at hand. You've attained a certain level of mastery in many abilities, such as walking, driving, sitting, standing, doing the dishes, reading, and talking, so you may not give these tasks a lot of conscious attention. In fact, much of the attention you spend is, for the most part, automatic and paid without your conscious awareness.

On the other hand, a certain amount of attention is consciously controlled, and this is the attention I want to address. It's called *intentional attention*. This is the attention you purposefully allocate to things you deem important, whether they are tasks you want to focus on, studies you want to pursue, talents you want to cultivate, projects you want to complete, or relationships you want to deepen.

Attention is something that you can train yourself to use more purposefully so you can reclaim that which you might otherwise give away unconsciously or unintentionally due to mental habits, distractions, or multitasking.

There is a true advantage to becoming more conscious of this limited resource of attention, and once you do, you can train yourself to harness the power of it. Cultivating intentional attention is the key to fully engaging in the world around you and empowering yourself and those you choose to share it with.

The Power of Intention

We are only beginning to recognize the power of intentional attention, and in some ways it is the scientific community leading the way. Ten years ago I met Dr. Masaru Emoto, a Japanese doctor of alternative medicine who was visiting Sedona, Arizona. He came to share the results of experiments he had done where he explored the effects of different types of attention on physical reality.

Emoto had chosen water as the focus of his research, both because water demonstrates a remarkable ability to contain and transfer information, and because the results of his research would also apply to human beings, since water comprises approximately 70 percent of the human body.

In the experiments, samples of water were intentionally exposed to particular words, images, thoughts, and music—some that were soothing and healing, and others that were chaotic or hateful. After the exposure, he quickly froze the water samples and each one formed into a crystalline structure that he examined under a microscope.

What was more important, Emoto explained, was not only the purity of the focused attention that was offered, but also the giver's ability to maintain an uninterrupted continuum of attention.

When the frozen samples were examined, Emoto observed that the degree of coherence in the formation of each ice crystal directly correlated with the *intention* which accompanied the *attention* directed toward the water sample. The more harmonious the thought, the more organized the structure of the ice crystals. The more violent the thought, the less structured and more chaotic were the crystals formed. Intention is information; attention is energy.

Emoto's research also showed that the distance between the object and the person was not a factor in the effect of attention. Each water sample responded equally to the continuum of attention, whether the person interacting with it was near or very far away.

Not only does the act of paying attention have a noticeable effect, the intention that accompanies it also has an effect. Attention and intention both have an effect undeterred by distance.

The Power of Thought

There was an experiment conducted in the 1970s by two scientists, E. Haraldsson and T. Thorsteinsson, which involved the growth of yeast cultures. They invited seven people to their lab to use only the power of intentional attention to affect the growth of 194 yeast cultures.

The subjects sat a yard and a half away from the petri dishes and focused their attention on them for 15 minutes with the intention of slowing down the yeast's growth. After the 15 minutes, the cultures were incubated for several more hours. The results showed that in 75 percent of the culture dishes, the yeast growth had slowed.

In an interview with Dr. Larry Dossey, who is a physician and the author of the book *Healing Words*, he talks about another study, a controlled, double-blind study, on the effect of prayer conducted in 1998 by the California Pacific Medical Center in San Francisco. In this study, prayers—intentional attention—were directed toward people with advanced AIDS. The results showed that those who were prayed for survived in greater numbers, became ill less often, and recovered faster than those who were not. And because the patients were unaware of whether they were or weren't in the group being prayed for, any placebo effect was eliminated.

In his own research into the power of healing words, Dossey went on to establish that even "when bacteria are prayed for, they tend to grow faster; when seeds are prayed for, they tend to germinate quicker; [and] when wounded mice are prayed for, they tend to heal faster. [These studies] eliminate all effects of suggestion and positive thinking," Dossey explained, "since . . . mice, seeds, and microbes presumably don't think positively!"

Dossey has studied the effects of prayer, or intentional attention, for over 30 years. Though he doesn't specify a particular formula for the perfect prayer, he does say that what is essential is the feeling that accompanies the attention, rather than the words that are used.

When you direct your attention toward a person or living thing, a current is created that has measurable effects. When the attention is accompanied by a feeling and an intention for well-being, you could consider this attention a current of love.

The Backster Effect

In 1966, Cleve Backster, a scientist best known for studying the consciousness of plants in order to answer the question of whether plants feel, attached lie detector electrodes to the leaves of his Dracaena plant in order to observe its reactions to various stimuli.

Backster made observations on the plant's responses to environmental threats, such as being burned, as well as its responses to opportunities for nourishment, such as being watered. The results were clear, but surprising: the plant not only responded to the stimulus, but also reacted to *thoughts* of harm or nourishment before any action actually took place! Backster called the plant's ability to sense its *primary perception*. He continued his experiments with lettuce, chicken eggs, yogurt, bacteria, brine shrimp, and sperm, and found that all life forms react to the presence of harm in their environments.

In an interview in the *Sun* magazine in July 1997, Backster commented, "It's very hard to eliminate the connection between the experimenter and the plants being tested. Even a brief association with the plants—just a few hours—is enough for them to become attuned to you. Then, even though you automate and randomize the experiment and leave the laboratory, guaranteeing you are entirely unaware of when the experiment starts, the plants will remain attuned to you, no matter where you go. At first, my partner and I would go to a bar a block away, but after a while we began to suspect that the plants were responding, not to the death of the brine shrimp, but to the rising and falling levels of excitement in our conversations."

Though his findings were controversial, they were given the name the *Backster Effect*, an effect that shows that not only are plants sentient, intelligent beings, but that they are also able to receive and give attention—and thus capable of creating a conscious connection with the attention givers.

Backster believed that plants are responsive and remarkably sensitive to both attention and intention, just as Emoto believed about water molecules. He imagined that if humans could be more in tune with these subtle communications, we could live more harmoniously with our environment and be more conscious of nourishment and toxicity affecting our planet.

Now we are discovering that living things in our environment, even if we are not aware of them, are in relationships with us, whether we consciously create these relationships or not!

Also, these living beings are affected by our negative and positive thoughts long before we put those thoughts into action. Our thoughts are powerful and go a long way toward determining the quality of our relationship with the world around us.

Every single thing—from people to animals to plants and even water molecules—is responsive to attention. Every living being responds to attention, whether that attention is negative or positive, and whether the attention given is on purpose or not.

As you move through your life in the coming days, begin to notice your relationship with the world you live in. Are you attentive to your environment and the people in it? Do you appreciate your environment? Do you walk with gratitude and care? Or do you rush through your days busy and distracted, too preoccupied to notice that you're in relationships with everyone and everything that surrounds you?

Intentional Attention

As we have seen from the previous studies, a drop of water, an animal, a plant, bacteria, and an open, receptive human being all have the potential to be affected by attention and intention. The implications of these and other studies with similar findings are huge! For years, people have talked about our ability to manifest our own reality. What we are beginning to understand is that, through intentional attention, we have the power to encourage or discourage those around us to flourish. Just by your thinking about something or someone, a response of some sort is summoned, even if the object of your attention is unaware they are being paid attention to, and even if what you are paying attention to is far away.

When you give your natural, nonjudgmental attention to someone or something, you are sending a very powerful message: "I see you. I hear you. I am considering you. I care for you. I love you." Attention that is given without condition could be considered a current of love. It joins you, the subject, and what is being paid attention to, the object, in a particular moment of time and space.

At the opposite end of this spectrum, there is contracted attention. This type of attention is veiled with conditions that accompany it. The expression of it can be any of these: expectant, distracted, dismissive, competitive, fixated, obsessive, perverted, scrutinizing, critical, judgmental, jealous, aggressive, hateful, argumentative, bullying, assuming, or angry. This type of attention can have a harmful effect on anything it's focused on, including when we focus it on ourselves. This is why it's important to examine the intention that accompanies your attention.

With this in mind, you can examine the quality of attention that you give to what truly matters to you: your body, your kids, your partner, your friends, your family, and your goals. Consider the attention you give your food, your home, your garden, the environment, the Earth, your hobbies, your clothes, your pets, your occupation, the news, politics, nature, people in need, people who seem more fortunate than you, and people who seem less fortunate than you.

It's probable that the quality of attention you offer in each moment falls somewhere along a spectrum—one that ranges from natural, unconditional, and expansive attention to judgmental, clinging, and contracted attention.

Attention Deficit

It's also important to consider the constancy and quality of the attention itself. For instance, if you pay partial attention to someone or something or are easily distracted, this can diminish the true engagement between you and the object of your attention. You know the scenario: Perhaps you've been sharing a meal with a friend who, in the middle of your dinner conversation, picks up her phone and checks her e-mail or texts. Perhaps there's a co-worker who is easily distracted while you are trying to get him to focus on a project or a problem. How do you feel when someone you're with is unable to focus?

Attention is so powerful that, when you neglect a relationship or withdraw your attention from something or someone by either ignoring or dismissing them, they can be harmed, sometimes even fatally.

The award-winning yet deeply disturbing film *The Dying Rooms* depicts just how essential loving attention is to the preservation of life. The documentary was set in China where, in 1978, a law was passed banning couples from raising more than one child. The taxation was exorbitant for those who had more than one child, and healthy male children were often preferred. It was all part of a family-planning policy that began to be formally phased out in 2015.

The film's title refers to a situation found in some Chinese state-run orphanages, institutions where a parent would drop off their baby girl or a child with disabilities shortly after birth. Though these children were fed, bathed, clothed, and kept safe, they needed more attention than that. Their cries for being held and for being paid attention to were repeatedly ignored. After some time, the babies would stop crying, and eventually they would stop thriving and engaging with life altogether.

While the dying rooms of China are an extreme example of the devastation that results from neglect, most of us have experienced being shunned or ignored, whether on purpose or simply because those around us were too distracted to offer their attention.

In his book *The Principles of Psychology*, the pioneering 19th-century psychologist William James described this experience as one of being "cut dead." He wrote:

> If no one turned round when we entered, answered when we spoke, or minded what we did, but if every person we met "cut us dead," and acted as if we were non-existing things, a kind of rage and impotent despair would ere long well up in us, from which the cruelest bodily tortures would be a relief; for these would make us feel that, however bad might be our plight, we had not sunk to such a depth as to be unworthy of attention at all.

Attention enlivens and affects all things, and in its absence one can experience a kind of slow death. And while most of us are sensitive to the disregard of others toward us, which we truly can't control, what we can control is our own ability to pay attention to what really matters to us.

When you neglect what is important to you, notice whether this neglect is obvious or subtle, and whether or not it is done purposefully. Often, we are neglectful not because we plan to be, but simply because we are distracted. Imagine, though, what the implications of neglect can be on the people or things we care about. Whether we allow ourselves to be distracted at home, at work, or from our goals, our inattention—purposeful or not—has an effect.

Separation and Stress

As a newborn, you had no ideas or notions about who you were, yet you were attentive and full of potential. Your nature was radiant, and your presence was one of joy, peacefulness, and love. Your sense of who you were, unlike that of an adolescent or adult, included *everything around you*. When you looked at the world— your mother, your father, the mobile over your crib, your food, the sky, everything—it was all a part of you. You saw it without separation. You were the world and all was well. This is the nature of an infant's brain.

Then you grew up, and your brain did, too. Little by little, there was a subject and object split. Life was no longer about "us" but about "I," "me," and "mine." You became concerned about your relationship with everything and everyone else. You have to be taught to share with the "others," because now there *are* others.

When you see everyone and everything in the world as separate from you, you develop a different relationship. You develop aversions and attractions. Your desires become more evident, and some are met while others aren't. And, as one of my teachers, the late Dr. David Simon, often said, "Stress is caused by anything getting in the way of your desires being met."

Stress occurs not only by desires not being met, but also from a variety of sources—mental, physical, emotional, and environmental. Stress begins to accumulate and compound in your nervous system. You might not notice it at first, but left unaddressed, stress can create chronic mental, physical, and emotional conditions. Those will get your attention at some point.

I use the analogy of dust landing on a glass table to illustrate the way stress accumulates and affects your nature. In my home in Sedona, as the sun shines through the windows in the morning, the dust is illuminated as it whirls and floats and ultimately lands on my glass coffee table. Over time, as the dust continues to accumulate, it mutes the transparency and the reflectivity of the glass. I barely notice it until I pick up my meditation timer and see the sharp contrast between the clear, untouched table under the timer and the dusty area around it. In order to restore the reflective and transparent nature of the glass, I have to wipe the dust from the table.

It's important to address the stress in your life and its effect on your attention—not only your ability to pay attention, but the overall lens through which you see the world. When your body reacts to a stressful situation, it sends out hormones that sharpen your attention and can even help you perform better. However, if you are constantly stressed and these hormones are constantly pumping into your system, it can affect your brain's ability to pay attention. This can affect your short-term memory and make you less able to focus and more easily distracted.

Chronic stress can also create mental habits: ways of thinking that make you more judgmental, anxious, depressed, frustrated, ashamed, or even angry. With stress, your relationships with the world and everyone and everything in it can soon become less friendly, less open, and less harmonious. It will also change the way you see yourself and your place in the world, and ultimately affect the quality and continuity of the attention you are able to direct toward people and things that matter to you.

You can't go through life completely avoiding stress—it's just not possible. But you can keep up with it. Fortunately, a daily meditation practice along with living more mindfully will prevent stress from building up and creating problems. Not only will these practices help you be more aware of what is actually causing you stress so you can avoid it or make a change, but also they reduce the actual effects of stress on the mind and body.

There are many ways to keep that table dusted, so to speak. It's important to get plenty of sleep, eat nourishing foods, align your daily routine with that of nature, be more body-aware, find fulfilling work, volunteer, eliminate toxic relationships, notice and change your negative internal dialogue, and set boundaries between work life and home life. Remember to pray, read, say what you mean, breathe deeply, listen to music, dance, move, walk, do yoga, exercise, laugh, and have fun. Spend quality time with friends and family, find a community that supports you in your spiritual pursuits, spend time with your pets, be creative, journal, do random acts of kindness, and be kind to yourself. To reduce your stress, it's important to be honest with yourself. Examine your lifestyle habits and make some adjustments by incorporating some of these suggestions so you live with clarity and presence and create relationships with the world and yourself.

The Mastery of Attention

Now that you are glimpsing the power of the currency of your attention, it's time to become more aware of how you use it. No one can master your attention for you. You are the one in charge of it. It is yours alone. You can become ridiculously in charge of your attention, and you can start right now by *paying attention to what you are paying attention to.*

When you think of someone who is considered a master of his or her craft, whether he or she is a botanist, physicist, novelist, cyclist, chef, dancer, musician, gardener, artist, or healer, consider that they have also had to become masters of their attention.

Mastery of your attention is a skill you can develop, and one that will impact every area of your life. What separates mastery from mediocrity in any endeavor is the ability to remain present emotionally and physically, even when confronted with the very same distractions and interferences that all of us face. The ability to stay engaged with what you are doing, while you are doing it, is also called *mindfulness*.

Mindfulness is a buzzword these days, even though the practice of mindfulness meditation has been around since the 5th century B.C.E., when Gautama Buddha was alive and teaching in India. Mindfulness is an English translation of the Pali word *sati*, which means awareness or attention, and its use is relatively new in the Western vernacular.

The term mindfulness can refer to either the formal practice of mindfulness meditation or to a state of mind and way of living. Living mindfully is when you purposely engage your non-judgmental attention with what is arising in each moment, with kindness and alertness. You can focus on your surroundings or on what you are doing, feeling, thinking, or saying. To be mindful means you are fully engaged, fully present, and welcoming what comes without judgment.

Any one of us can be mindful. You don't have to be a Buddhist, or a good meditator, or especially wise. Mindfulness and your ability to sustain your attention can be cultivated deliberately through mindfulness practices and meditation.

Attending to Attention

Your natural attention is the currency of love, so it is important to take a look at the way you allot your attention to the people, places, and things that you consider to be most important to you. What enhances or detracts from your ability to pay attention? Perhaps you are distracted by your internal dialogue, your physical sensations, or your emotions. Perhaps your attention is siphoned away by thoughts, obsessions, or compulsions. What distracts you in your environment? Consider the media, electronic devices, a co-worker, pets, or even clutter.

Attention can be limited not only due to distractions but also feelings of fatigue, being overloaded, and a habitual attitude of negativity. When you are stressed out, you can tend to be reactive rather than responsive, and this can make it easy for the bells and buzzes of different electronic devices to call you off task. Consider that the more stressed out you are, the more reactive you are to the stimuli around you, and the less able you are to consciously direct your attention.

Notice the quality of attention that you tend to have: Is it clear and expanded or contracted? Is it kind or critical? Do you focus your attention on that which inspires you, or do you give ongoing negative attention to a particular person or situation, such as bringing up past relationships or fixating on faults and imperfections?

Without judging yourself, simply witness and explore your emotional state based on what and how you pay attention. Notice the quality of the various interactions you have with your loved ones, your co-workers, your neighbors, service workers, and others you encounter in your day. Notice how you pay attention and your continuum of attention. Notice how who and what you pay attention to affects you. Also, notice how you feel when you are receiving kind attention from others.

The exercises in this book will help you pay attention to your attention. You'll first monitor your ability to pay attention and where you tend to focus it. Then you'll examine how that which you give your attention to affects your body, mind, and emotions. Next, you'll explore the intentions that accompany your attention. Finally, you'll be introduced to keys to help you create a new relationship to that which distracts you, so you can be fully present to what matters to you. You are responsible for your attention and are the only one who can transform the way you use it.

The Examination of Attention

The questions that follow are designed to illuminate your ability to manage your attention as you notice what you pay attention to, how you pay attention, and the quality of your attention. Read through each question and either use them as journal prompts or simply reflect upon them as you go about your day. This inquiry will reveal to you the way you use the currency of your attention.

Ask yourself:

- *Do I give enough attention to the people, activities, and things that are important to me?*

- *How does someone or something respond when I give him/her/it my undivided attention? How do they respond when I am distracted in his/her/its presence? (You might be too distracted to notice!)*

- *Do I pay attention to and listen to my inner knowing?*

- *How do I feel physically—and where in my body do I feel it—when I judge, feel spiteful, or have ill will toward a particular person or situation?*

- *How do I feel—and where in my body do I feel it—when I offer loving and supportive attention to a family member, a friend, or a stranger?*

- *How do I feel—and where in my body do I feel it—when someone ignores me, disregards my requests, or is generally not present when they're with me?*

- *How do I feel—and where in my body do I feel it—when I am truly being paid attention to?*

- *Do I often multitask or am I able to sustain an uninterrupted continuum of attention?*

- *What external stimulus most distracts me? (My phone? My relationship? The people or objects in my environment?)*

- *What internal stimulus distracts me? (My obsessions? My daydreams? My grudges? My limiting beliefs? Body sensations?)*

- *How long can I engage and be present with someone without looking at an electronic device?*

- *Do I feel a sense of rushing even when there are no deadlines and nowhere to go?*

With this inquiry, you'll be more conscious of how you want to spend this valuable currency of attention.

You might get frustrated as you see that you live in a world full of distractions and potential addictions. And, yes, the contemporary culture seems to encourage the half-hearted way some of us attend to the world around us. By noticing what distracts and detours you, you can begin to create some boundaries around them to reclaim your focus.

Here are some tips to reclaim your attention:

- Set your priorities. Make a commitment to give your attention to what matters to you, whether it's your body, your relationships, your creativity, your work, your family, your pets, your plants, your spiritual life, or your environment. The ability to fully engage in a relationship with others and attend to yourself is expressed in your ability to listen, to love, to connect, and to respond in compassionate and meaningful ways.

- Practice fully engaging in a conversation. Mindfully listen and stay connected as the person in front of you speaks. Don't interrupt, or assume. Simply be present. When you respond, speak mindfully and with your full attention.

- Get to know your body. Listen with the same loving attention you offer to others. Ask yourself, "How do I feel when I focus on this?" The "this" in this case can be anything: a goal, a memory, a co-worker, your family, your pet, a project, social media, a problem at work, nature, a television show, a news article, or any activity you are engaged in. Choose to focus more on that which nourishes you.

- Go analog. Stop sleeping with your phone. Instead, use a clock or watch. Don't start the day in emergency mode. Create a relaxing morning routine, one where you can be present and calm. This will establish a restful response as you embark on your day.

- Take some time to unplug from your devices and social media—whether a few hours a day, or one day a week. Create boundaries around what distracts you. Make time to be completely available to your three dimensional reality. Uninterrupted time is when creativity and inspiration can arise and your real-life relationships can flourish.

- Get a dose of nature. Research shows that a 20 minute walk can improve attentional issues. The natural world is a conduit for connecting to reality. It brings you to your senses and can charm your attention. This gives your brain a break from endless to-do lists and habitual thinking patterns that keep you distracted.

You can reclaim and increase the power of your attention and pay full attention, on purpose, to whom and what you choose. Harnessing your ability to pay attention will restore the relational space between you and who and what you focus on. Your attention is powerful, and you can be in charge of it when you set your mind to it.

Chapter 2

Attention in Training

*By being with yourself . . . by watching yourself in your
daily life with alert interest, with the intention to understand
rather than to judge, in full acceptance of whatever may emerge,
because it is there, you encourage the deep to come to the surface
and enrich your life and consciousness with its captive energies.
This is the great work of awareness; it removes obstacles and
releases energies by understanding the nature of life and
mind. Intelligence is the door to freedom and alert
attention is the mother of intelligence.*

—NISARGADATTA MAHARAJ

Now that you are focusing your attention on how you pay
attention and are noticing the effects your attention has on others—and how theirs affects you—you are probably more alert to
the power that attention wields.

In this chapter, we are going to explore practices to train your
attention. Meditation, especially mindfulness meditation, can
reveal how well you pay attention and illuminates the intentions
that accompany your attention. It will also help you hone your
ability to sustain your attention.

Scientists are now confirming what the mystics and yogis have
known for thousands of years: you can change the way you think,
the way you make choices, and the way you experience life by

training your attention with practices such as mindfulness and meditation. That's because these practices have a direct effect on the structure and function of your brain, especially in the areas of the insula, the hippocampus, and the amygdala—areas related to increased self-awareness, self-control, compassion, enhanced focus, learning, and memory, as well as reduced reactivity in the stress response.

Research also shows that what you pay attention to, both the negative and the positive, can have lasting effects on your brain structure. For example, stressful and disturbing thoughts have a direct effect on the brain, as do positive and inspiring thoughts. By virtue of what you focus your attention on, you activate different parts of your brain's circuitry and can change its structure. There's a saying about the brain: what fires together, wires together.

Your brain is malleable—it is not a static organ, but a collection of neural pathways that respond and reorganize based on what you pay attention to. Even the well-worn highways forged by habit and inattention can be abandoned and be replaced by new pathways that support your ability to sustain your attention. This innate ability of the brain to change its structure and wiring is called *neuroplasticity*. Research supports that you can purposely create a new way of interfacing with your world with what is called *self-directed neuroplasticity*—the practice of intentionally changing your brain by means of controlled attention and intention. This is exactly what is occurring during the practice of various types of meditation.

Return from India

In 1990, I was a resident at the mind-body health center run by the Transcendental Meditation organization outside of Boston, where Deepak Chopra was the medical director. There, I fell in love with *ayurveda*, the science of life and longevity—an ancient healing approach from India that includes massages; yoga; herbal remedies; taste, color, and sound therapy; diet; daily routine; and meditation to create balance and reduce stress in the mind and body. I worked, lived, and meditated alongside more than a dozen other residents, studying with *vaidyas* (ayurvedic physicians) and *jyotishis* (those who study the planets and light and their effects) who were visiting from India.

A couple of years later, when Deepak was invited to California to head up a new mind-body health center, I moved there to help. I was the education director, directing mind-body health programs and teaching mantra meditation classes. After a few years, I sensed it was time to move on, although I didn't know where I'd go. Maybe I'd travel.

One evening, I joined some friends at a hotel in Orange County, California, to meet a visiting Indian guru who was touring the United States. You may have heard of her, she's hugged millions of people all over the world. She's Mata Amritanandamayi, or Amma, known as the hugging saint.

Upon entering the conference room, I felt permeated with peacefulness, even though there were hundreds of people milling around. Many of them were focused on the woman in white sitting in the front of the room. The longer I watched her, the more awestruck I became by the tireless loving attention she gave to each of the visitors who came to see her and get a hug.

While sitting with her, I felt immediately soothed, and even blessed. I wanted to be around her more. I imagined visiting her in India and while there, exploring the birthplace of the meditation and ayurveda practices I had fallen in love with. I immediately bought a plane ticket to India once I got home, and then I got my visa. I was to leave in a month.

I became a resident in Amma's practice community, a traditional ashram in South India. She was the guru there. *Guru* means teacher, but Hindu scriptures translate the word as "dispeller of darkness." I was assigned a bunk bed in a large women's dorm over the meditation hall. There were no bedsheets, only a bamboo mat on the plywood bed. Though it was hot and sticky day and night, I was excited to once again be part of a community, people who have traveled from all over the world who shared a common desire: to thin out their ego, find inner peace, and ultimately to become enlightened.

The more time I spent with Amma, the more I wanted to realize the divine in myself and in all things. I wanted to see the world as Amma describes it:

See every object

as your beloved deity.

When holding a book,

handling clothes, or opening a door,

mentally bow to the beloved divinity

who stands before you.

This is how she does it, I thought. She gives everyone and everything her undivided attention. She recognizes the field of love shining through each and every one of us, and in all forms of creation. She has described it as, "Everything seems permeated with divinity. Every blade of grass and every sand particle is filled with divine energy."

The days were punctuated with chores, such as doing laundry, cleaning floors, and chopping fruits and vegetables. Most of my time, however, was spent sitting on the concrete floor in the large meditation hall, either singing devotional songs or in meditation with Amma and the rest of the residents.

Mantra meditation was a surefire way to lessen the dominance of my mental activity and the distraction of my physical whereabouts. It allowed me to transcend everyday reality. In fact, the word *transcend* means to "go beyond," which is exactly what would happen for me in meditation. My awareness of that which exists in time and space (thoughts, feelings, body sensations, other people, places, things, etc.) would merge into the underlying vast awareness of existence itself: a silent, boundless realm. It is that same essence that flows through all existence: you, me, your body, my body, animals, plants, everything! (You'll learn a mantra meditation later in the book so you can experience it for yourself.)

Mantra meditation had long been my go-to meditation; I knew it was a reliable way of connecting with internal bliss and peace. However, once the meditation period was over, I was again distracted by thoughts of past experiences, concerns about my future, and curiosity about what other people were doing. This inability to focus was unsettling to me. While I was certainly more attentive and present after a meditation than I was before I began, the distractions were annoying. I wanted to be present to the wonder and beauty of creation at *all* times. I wanted to be able to focus on the people in front of me and what I was experiencing.

Sitting Practice: Zazen

Six months later, when I returned from India, I was at a crossroads. I could either continue my spiritual pursuits, or I could get a "real" job. I applied to a handful of startup mind-body health centers and educational facilities and went on interviews, but none of the positions seemed like a fit. So I made my decision: I would move to a Zen Buddhist practice center and continue my inward journey.

The place I chose, Yokoji Zen Mountain Center, is a quiet, traditional practice center in the middle of the mountains in Southern California. Japanese Zen priest, Taizan Maezumi Roshi, who in the '80s was a pioneer of American Zen, founded the center. Tom, my ex-boyfriend and traveling partner, introduced me to it. He had settled at the Zen center to deepen his meditation practice a few years before. When I'd worked at the Chopra Center, I would often go there on my weekends off; now, returning to it, the place gave me a sense of safety and support.

For the next two years, my home was a very small wooden cabin perched on the hillside. It was just barely big enough for a twin mattress and my few things. The bathroom was a long walk away down a hill covered in pine needles. The cool beauty of the mountainside forest contrasted with the crowded hot ashram I had just left. It was physically spacious and quiet, and I felt immediately nourished.

Here, there was no religion, nothing to believe in. There were no gods, no mantras, and no miracles. Instead, there was only practice—the practice of being present both in meditation and to everyday moments. In meditation, the emphasis was not on transcending, but instead on being mindful and being present.

Mindfulness is a generic term for what is an essentially Buddhist practice. However, most Buddhists do not set out with the sole goal of being mindful. In addition to focus, they want to attain *satori*, or enlightenment. This is done by looking deeply into the nature of reality: the nature of one's self, and that of everything else. (Zen masters say that it's impossible to convey satori in words. It is an experience beyond duality, beyond the separation of subject and object. It is instead an attainment of a new perception of reality, a realization of that unity which underlies all things.) You need to be attentive to look deeply into anything.

Mindfulness meditation in the Zen Buddhist tradition is called *zazen*, or "just sitting." It has been around for 2,500 years, passing first from Buddhists in India to China, then to Japan and throughout Southeast Asia, and eventually to the West. Unlike the mantra meditation I'd been practicing, posture really matters in zazen; in fact, *everything* matters in this practice. It is important to maintain a straight spine, imagining the top of your head pushing toward the ceiling. You slightly tuck your chin and relax your body. You can choose to sit in one of a variety of cross-legged positions on top of a *zafu* (a round meditation cushion), which is placed on a *zabuton* (a square meditation mat filled with cotton) on the floor. Or you can kneel while resting your rear on a wooden *seiza* bench. If none of these positions work for you, then sitting in a chair will suffice.

Also unlike the mantra meditation practices I had been used to, in zazen the eyes are just slightly open—what I call "capped"— softly gazing toward the floor a few feet in front of you. The hands are in your lap, positioned in a *mudra* (which means "gesture"). Your dominant hand holds the other hand, both palms up, with knuckles overlapping and thumbs slightly touching to form an oval.

The focus of your attention in zazen is on your breathing. You breathe through your nose and engage your attention on the sensations of breathing in and out. Every time you notice your attention is no longer on the breath and you've been distracted by another concern or thought, you simply return your attention again to the breath. There is no need for judgment or self-recrimination whenever this happens; instead, you simply refocus.

Physical sensations can be a distraction too, especially during the long retreats. When they are present, you simply give your undivided attention to the nature of the sensations themselves as they arise, then dissipate. My simple guidelines are: welcome everything, resist nothing, and expect nothing.

This back-and-forth focus—from breath to distraction and back—is the training of your attention, and this goes on for the entire meditation session. (You will find instructions for this simple breath-awareness practice at the end of this chapter.)

Staying Present and Bearing Witness

The practice of zazen cultivates what many teachers call a "witnessing awareness." As you witness the activity of body and mind without clinging to preferences, without expecting anything, without resisting, and without labeling it, you become intimate with it while being less affected by the experiences and sensations you're engaged with.

In our very early morning meditations, we'd gather in silence in the *zendo* (meditation hall) to meditate by the light of a candle's flame. The doors would be wide open, and in the cold winter months, as dawn broke and the sun's first rays hit the mountaintops that surrounded us, freezing air would descend into the valley and through those open doors. It would get colder and colder as we sat in stillness, watching our breath cloud the air. Sometimes, field mice seeking shelter from the cold would run right over our laps to reach the other side of the hall. We were not to move when this happened, but instead to silently bear witness to the sensation and notice our own reactions to it.

I didn't check out, as I sometimes did when practicing mantra meditation. Instead, I learned how to *stay present* to the ever-changing world of emotional, physical, and mental activity. Staying present means that when a sensation arises, you attend to how it actually *feels*. For instance, when your foot falls asleep, pain shoots through your knees or your back, or your face feels really cold, you remain present to the experience. *What does my foot falling asleep feel like? What does pain feel like? From where does it arise?*

It's important to avoid getting caught up in an idea or story about a sensation or judging what you feel. Instead, bring your attention to the sensation; this is called *bearing witness*. You may even feel as if you are watching your experiences. As you become less attached to all this activity, your relationship with it changes. You'll know it—and yourself—much more intimately.

Even in a perfectly comfortable environment, it's natural to become distracted or agitated during meditation, or to suddenly realize that you've gone off on a mental tangent or daydream. When thoughts, emotions, physical sensations, and distractions occur—and they will—your job is simply to bring your attention back to the focus, without judgment or self-recrimination. Beating yourself up does absolutely no good in any meditation. Like training a puppy to stay in the yard, keep sweetly calling your attention back until eventually it learns where home is.

My own mental journeys at the Zen center ranged from the mystical to the ridiculously mundane, as I'd catch myself asking questions of some unseen source: *Who am I? Why am I here? Will I ever be enlightened? Shall I get someone to help me in the kitchen? Has the bread risen? What is the meaning of life? Am I lovable? What will we have for dinner tomorrow, with all the new guests coming? What's wrong with me? Does everyone have thoughts like these? Will I ever be happy? How much longer can I afford to stay here? Am I too fat? Should I shave my head?* My internal dialogue was never-ending, nonsensical, and self-indulgent.

My attention was also hijacked by the past. I'd feel regretful that I hadn't made the right choices or done enough. In my mind's eye, I would relive my travels through India, seeing the stray dogs and sacred cows, the orphaned boys and girls who formed gangs and slept in train stations, and the sights and sounds of life in the ashram. I revisited my decision to elope when I was in the Army, thought about past boyfriends, and fantasized about finding the love of my life. I also recognized that I was sidetracked by the personal relationships of the other trainees. I'd speculate about the rigor of their practices and their stages of enlightenment. Then I'd realize how far my attention had drifted, and refocus on my breath.

Emotions naturally accompany thought, so I'd often go from thinking I was very spiritual to feeling sorry for myself. It was a journey of highs to lows, from bliss to shame, and from hopeful to upset, all within a few hours each day. When a truly powerful emotion actually reared its head, I had a sense that truly feeling it would be unbearably painful and I might not be able to stop crying if I let myself start. (That's when I realized that this spiritual path was not for sissies!)

With time, I became able to stay present to sensations without reactivity. Soon, I felt safe enough to follow an emotion as it came into existence, moved through my body, and then dissipated. I noticed that an emotion didn't stay long. There would be a beginning, middle, and end; it wasn't going to kill me. Instead, each became an interesting phenomenon to witness, just like sensations in the body and the movement of my breath.

All of these—thoughts, emotions, and physical sensations—were wonderful opportunities to bear witness and return my attention to my breath. Although I'd been meditating for years, zazen opened my eyes to how little control I had over the wanderings and musings of my own mind. Starting again and again, it was like watching ping pong as my mind bounced: thought, breath, thought, emotion, breath.

It took me a while to learn that and to remember that mindfulness is not a destination to be reached, but a deliberate moment-by-moment practice. Indeed, this is why it is called a *practice*.

Rituals

In a Zen community, almost every aspect of daily living is ritualized. There are formal and specific ways to enter the zendo and rules about to whom and when to bow, how to sit while meditating, when and how to meet with a teacher, when and what to chant, how to go from sitting to standing to walking, what to wear while working—and even when and how to bathe.

I've come to learn that rituals are an opportunity to regain presence and attention. A ritual is a moment in time when we perform a set action, and we pay attention to that action. Rituals anchor our attention and clarify our intention. Most people have them, whether they are as mundane as making a cup of tea, or as devout as reading a passage in a holy book. Rituals are perfect moments of mindfulness and opportunities to train your attention.

Cooking, too, has its own set of rituals, which I would learn in my work at the Zen center. In addition to the regular practice of zazen, residents of the Zen center were assigned a work practice, or *samu*. Mostly they were simple daily tasks like chopping vegetables, washing dishes, working on a website, stocking the store, vacuuming the zendo, or cleaning the bathrooms. Like meditation, samu is an opportunity to increase your ability to pay attention.

I was assigned to help the *tenzo*, the head cook, plan and make the meals for the residents and guests. Each morning, at the 4:40 A.M. ringing of the gong, I'd grab my long black robe and carefully walk downhill in the dark, making my way to the kitchen. Before starting to prepare breakfast, I'd light a candle and an incense stick at the altar hanging on the kitchen wall, and chant a kitchen blessing. With the intention to be present and mindful, I'd quietly make enough coffee and tea for the *sangha*, the "community."

Inevitably, before the tea was finished brewing, a practitioner would wander through the kitchen door in search of his or her morning cup. I'd come to expect the daily arrival of Kokyo from Switzerland, whose ritual was to drink her cup of black coffee with an early morning cigarette as she sat under the pine tree just outside the kitchen.

A few months after I arrived, the tenzo left, and soon afterward I became tenzo. Now, instead of simply helping with meals, I was in charge of planning menus, shopping for supplies, and preparing daily meals for the residents and 30 or so guests who visited in any given week. Each morning, I'd chop fruit while the cereal cooked. I'd light the woodstove in the dining room so it would be comfortable. Once everything was ready to be served, I would put on my robe and silently join the others in meditation in the zendo.

The role of tenzo—which, translated from Japanese, means "heavenly monk"—is an important one in a monastery, second only to the *sensei*, or teacher. The position comes with very specific guidelines, most of which were loosely outlined in the 13th century by Zen Master Dogen in *Instructions for the Zen Cook*. In this short manual on how to prepare meals for fellow monks, Dogen drew a parallel between the preparation of daily meals and the "cooking" or "refining" of one's life. The rules are simple: attend to what you are doing while you are doing it, with nonjudgmental awareness. His instructions were to "put your awakened mind to work" and to have an attitude of joy and appreciation for having received the task. He said that cooking and caring for other people were as important as meditation and chanting.

I wanted to heed Dogen's instructions and engage in my duties as tenzo wholeheartedly, with a pure, focused mind—but I very quickly discovered I was far from mindful. Samu was simple, but not easy. As much as I wanted to be present and to attend to the task at hand, whether chopping carrots or kneading dough, I was otherwise occupied with daydreams or mental and emotional field trips.

Just like I would experience in zazen, instead of attending to what I was doing, my experience of *here, now, and this* was continually interrupted by thoughts of *there, then, and that*—other places, other times, and other things, as well as by the emotions that accompanied these mental excursions.

We all go on these trips; but no matter the situation or surroundings, we have opportunities to better harness our attention as we do simple, ordinary activities like going on a walk.

Going for a Walk

Mindful walking is a simple and universal practice for developing greater calmness, present-moment awareness, and clarity of mind. It cultivates mindfulness in action and is a great practice for those who can't or won't sit still, or can't find the time to meditate formally. There are two ways to go for a walk: you can be distracted and thinking of another place and time, or you can be present to the sounds in the environment and the sensations of walking.

At the Zen center, a formal walking meditation known as *kinhin* was practiced between our sitting periods in the zendo. When the bell signaled the end of a meditation period, we'd stand, bow, turn left; then, at the sound of wooden blocks being clacked, we'd walk clockwise around the inside of the zendo for about 10 minutes. Kinhin is used to get circulation in the legs going again, as well as to shake off the tension that builds up due to extended inactivity. (It's also a chance to duck out and use the restroom, or get your place in line for meeting with the teacher.) Kinhin probably originated in ancient India as the first Buddhist practitioners mindfully walked around monuments, called *stupas*.

Walking meditation can be practiced formally or informally. You can practice it informally anywhere, even walking in a parking lot or up and down grocery store aisles. You can also practice it formally. You'll have to choose a place to walk, indoors or out, such as a hiking trail, a city sidewalk, or a meditation room—anywhere you can walk comfortably. Do this practice for a set period of time; anywhere from five to ten minutes is fine.

In mindful walking, you focus your nonjudgmental attention simultaneously on the sensations of stillness and movement, including the steps of your foot. Be in the experience of walking. Attend to the micromovements your body makes to keep its balance with each step. Whenever you notice you've gotten distracted, you return your attention, without judgment, to the sensation of walking.

I've found walking meditations to be invaluable in the creative writing retreats that I facilitate. During these retreats, we unplug for the weekend. We eat in silence and we write in silence. This allows for the mental spaciousness required for creative impulses to arise.

Some people have told me that they feel self-conscious when doing this, especially when we practice in a public place. They're embarrassed to do what they call the "zombie walk," which is walking slowly with their eyes toward the ground. However, I think the real zombie walk is when we walk with our heads down, too distracted to notice where we are and who is around us because we are checking an electronic device—consumed by concerns of what other people in other places are doing. With that type of zombie walk, we can miss the clouds in the sky, the birdsongs, creative impulses, or the opportunity for chance encounters with friends or strangers. We can miss the magic of our real lives.

The Most Important Thing

There's a saying (which has been attributed to Buddha, Tolstoy, and even to Deepak Chopra) that proclaims, "The most important moment is *now*; the most important activity is *the one you are engaged in*; and the most important person is *the one in front of you*." What a challenge to put that into practice!

When weekend visitors and retreatants arrived at the Zen center, some simply curious and others committed practitioners, instead of welcoming them or being attentive for a few minutes, I'd busily rush around. My "I know" mind would imagine that I already knew who they were, why they were there, and what they were going to say. In short, I dismissed them, and instead of meeting them, I met only my ideas *about* them.

In fact, I was uncomfortable *being* and more comfortable *doing*. Eventually, I had to confront whatever it was that kept me from connecting—and, like everything else, it only changes with attention.

As the days and months passed, I was more able to sustain my attention on the present moment, whether I was walking, meditating, chanting, or chopping. Also, I was more able to be more present for others and for myself, whether I was meeting new guests in the kitchen and giving them my full attention or being compassionate toward myself when weathering the storms of emotional pain.

After almost two years, I was ready to reemerge into society. A new adventure awaited. I was ready to see the world through the eyes of love.

Your Basic Training

If you believe that you can't meditate, or you aren't good at it, or you're not able to have the experiences you've heard or read about, I can tell you with certainty that *everyone* can meditate. I've never met anyone who can't, and I've taught meditation to thousands of people. There are plenty of people who *won't* meditate for various reasons, mostly because they think they're too busy, it doesn't work for them right away, they fall asleep, or they can't quiet their mind. However, the ability to meditate is your birthright, just like your ability to sleep, breathe, love, and create.

Perhaps meditation began thousands of years ago, as the first people were intrigued by fire and light—gazing at the sun's movement, the stars in the night sky, or the communal fires. Maybe it began with questions about the world around them and their place in it, such as "What is all this?" or "Who am I?"

Meditation is a word that refers to many techniques and practices, both modern and ancient. All of them settle your nervous system, reduce stress, and train your brain to be more focused, more engaged, and less reactive. You've now heard about mindfulness, mantra, breath-awareness, and walking meditations. You might also know of visualization, contemplation, body scanning, chanting, compassion, vipassana, gratitude, loving-kindness, or insight. There are many, many other varieties, but when you examine them, you'll find that overall, meditation is a very simple practice. It's not easy, especially for those of us who are accustomed to multitasking, who are easily distracted, or who generally won't sit still, but the practice itself is simple.

I realize that paying attention on purpose is a difficult skill to master, even when the desire is there. This is, after all, why some of us head off to live in spiritual communities; they are places that provide an environment to become disciplined in certain practices while surrounded by others with similar intent. While not everyone has the ability (or the desire) to just pick up and leave for a monastery, you can reap the same benefits that I did by adopting the practices of meditation and mindfulness. I hope that the following information and guidelines will help you navigate these practices and the experiences that occur as you engage in them.

The Benefits of Daily Practice

With a regular daily practice of meditation, your attention will improve in three ways. You'll more easily:

- Sustain your focus on one thing at a time
- Be attentive to the present moment
- Gain more inner focus and self-awareness

When you are able to focus on one thing at a time, you'll find you are more available to yourself and to what is actually happening in your life. You can sustain your attention on a project, a person, or a situation that is important to you, instead of being distracted, doing too many things at once, or mentally checking out.

You'll also be more present to the actual experiences of your life instead of the ideas you have about your life. Though memories of the past and plans and desires for the future will still be a part of your world, they won't hijack your attention from the actual experience of the life you are living, right now, in real time. You'll learn to appreciate and savor the moments of your life when you are paying attention.

Meditation will also help you to be more self-aware. This means you'll be more present to what you think, how you pay attention, how you feel, and how you choose to respond to a situation.

Meditation will also help you to be more relaxed. It reduces the overactivation of the sympathetic nervous response, also known as the fight-or-flight response. Multiple studies show that during meditation, brain and body chemistry changes, allowing the parasympathetic nervous response (the rest-and-digest response) to reign. This creates healthy changes in circulation, immunity, and brain-wave patterns. The stress hormone, cortisol, decreases while feel-good hormones such as serotonin and oxytocin increase. You'll have access to more spaciousness between stimulus and response. And, when you do experience a stressful situation, you'll be able to recover quickly once the situation has passed.

Your reference point for navigating your life will no longer be influenced by the ever-changing world you live in; instead, you will be anchored by an internal centerpoint of peace. A stressful moment won't ruin your whole day. You'll be calmer, more resilient, and stable in the midst of change. I call it being *soul-centered*.

It may even feel as if you are living with a sense of a new normal, one where you are peaceful, creative, present, and living in real time, enjoying your real life. You will be the one in charge of where you put your attention. You'll decide what to focus on and attend to. This will give you more power.

It's important to remember: *knowing* about meditation and mindfulness will not give you these benefits; *doing it* will.

The Three Ingredients of Meditation

Almost every meditation practice requires three simple ingredients: your natural attention, an object to focus your attention on, and resolve to stay with the practice even when it gets challenging.

The practice of meditation cultivates well-being, increases vitality, and helps develop compassion, love, patience, generosity, and forgiveness toward yourself and others. It creates a strong, peaceful centerpoint from which to attend to life. However, you can't get the benefits of meditation unless you *do* it. So, meditation requires not only the discipline to set aside the time each day, but also a commitment to stick with the practice, even if you're bored or have difficulty sitting still.

Meditation is a radical act of self-love.

Take a moment and recall what it was that prompted you to buy this book. What are you hoping to discover or attain? Is it greater power, love, focus, peace, or contentment? What is your hope? This, combined with your determination to practice, is your *sankalpa*, which means "vow" in Sanskrit.

Now, let's talk about the quality of attention needed for meditation. Meditation doesn't require superhuman or intense powers of concentration. Instead, it requires your natural, bare, gentle attention. Try this simple exercise to experience what that feels like:

- *Bring your attention to your right hand. (You don't have to move it or look at it, simply focus your attention on it.)*

- *Notice whatever sensations are present. Feel them.*

- *Now, switch your focus to your left hand for a moment.*

- *Notice the sensations there.*

- *Now, switch back to the right.*

The way you focused your attention on the sensations of your hands is the way you'll focus on an object in your meditation. It's an easy, natural attention.

Yes, you might've gotten distracted and thought of other things, even during that short exercise. Don't worry, this is natural. At least you noticed it! And, just as easily as you were able to shift your focus from your right hand to your left and back again, you'll refocus again on the object of your meditation when you notice your attention has wandered. This practice is training you to pay attention to one thing at a time.

Now let's explore the various focuses you can use in meditation. Though there are some meditations that don't require a focus and ask you instead to be aware of the general panorama of what you experience with your eyes closed, most do suggest you attend to one. There are three main senses that you can use in meditation: hearing, feeling, and seeing.

You can focus on something tactile—such as the sensations you notice in your hands, or the feeling of exhaling and inhaling. You can focus on the sensations of moving, such as walking or doing yoga. You can even focus on an emotion, such as forgiveness, gratitude, compassion, or joy.

The focus of your meditation can also be visual. You could focus on a star in the night sky, or gaze softly at a candle flame. Or, you could visualize an image, a shape, or an icon in your mind's eye.

And, finally, the focus of meditation can be auditory. You can listen to a sound of nature, such as the ebb and flow of an ocean's waves or the subtle sounds of your own breath, or the sounds created by a gong or crystal bowls. You can also repeat a mantra or a prayer, either silently or aloud, or listen to them being spoken by others.

These are just some examples of the objects of focus used in the variety of meditation practices, new and old.

Where, When, and How to Meditate

Find a comfortable place to meditate, ideally indoors. Though it may seem like a romantic idea to meditate on a mountaintop, it isn't always practical or even desirable. Meditating outside introduces more disturbances, so I suggest you do yourself a favor and meditate where you can control the environment, at least in the beginning. Consider that in ancient times, most yogis practiced in caves. The idea here is that you can meditate almost anywhere that you will be relatively undisturbed. Turn off sounds, and turn off your phone. See if you can be present to life in the silence.

It's important to carve out some time in your schedule for meditation; if possible, make it the same time every day. The body likes rhythm. Morning is the best time to meditate, preferably shortly after you rise. As Deepak Chopra says, "Get up to sit down." You are probably pretty relaxed when you get up—unless you slept with your phone and looked at it before you even sat up, so don't do that! By meditating in the morning, you cultivate a responsive, relaxed, and attentive way to enter your day.

If you can, meditate twice a day, with the second meditation in the evening sometime between work and dinner. I call it "happy hour meditation." Make sure that it's at least three hours before bed. Meditation is not best practiced right before sleep, as it can sometimes increase alertness and vitality (although there are sleeping meditations you can do). If those times don't work for you, you can meditate before lunch. It's easier to meditate on a relatively empty stomach, so if you do eat, wait an hour afterward to meditate.

When your meditation period is over, take a moment or two to rest in stillness before you return to your daily routine. This is the integration period.

Make meditation a priority in your life and incorporate it into your daily routine. The purpose of meditation is to have a better life. It's a training that you can use in life to attend to what's important to you. Remember how important your attention is?

With it you can experience aha moments, be alert to coincidences, and notice the wonders that surround you.

Falling Asleep During Meditation

The deep rest you experience in meditation has many of the same effects as sleep. When asleep, your body releases stress, restores balance, and recharges its vitality.

During meditation, some new meditators feel their head bobbing up and down as if they are falling asleep. They probably aren't falling asleep but instead are in a deep state of relaxation—and they've probably never been that relaxed while still being awake! I call this bobbing "the new meditator's nod." It should stop after a couple weeks, once the body gets used to being that rested while sitting up.

That being said, everyone falls asleep once in a while in meditation. If you do, it simply means your body has accumulated fatigue and is taking the opportunity to rest. Meditation will always give you the most evolutionary, nourishing, and purifying experience. (If you often feel fatigued, you may need to adjust your routine and go to bed earlier.)

If you find yourself falling asleep frequently in meditation, be sure that you are sitting up, and consider meditating with your eyes slightly open. Another technique that helps with alertness is to lie down for about 10 minutes before your meditation period.

If you do fall asleep in meditation, once you wake up you can simply finish the meditation period or meditate for another five minutes.

Tips for Keeping Up Your Practice

Although meditation will make you think more clearly and be more focused, it is important to not try to clear your mind of thoughts in meditation. The nature of the mind is to think, just as the nature of your eye is to see. So in meditation, like in life, your mind will be busy with thoughts. Your attention will naturally drift from whatever you are supposed to be focused on without your even realizing it. Suddenly you become aware that you are paying attention to some sound in the environment or a litany of thoughts or a physical sensation.

Once you realize you have gotten distracted, your job is to return to the object of focus, again and again, all the while being gentle with yourself. This is the practice of training your attention. Over time, you'll find that you can sustain your attention for longer and longer.

Be sure to stay with the entire practice even if distractions persist, and even when you are restless or bored. This commitment to the practice is what diminishes the dominance of the reactivity center of the brain. By sitting through it, you will become more responsive, rather than reactive, in your life. Remember, meditation is a training.

Never judge your meditation by the experiences you have in meditation. Instead, realize that it is working even if you don't love the particular session you just had. In reality, it's the practice that matters, not your opinion of it. Anyway, the benefits show up when you are not meditating.

Breath-Awareness Meditation

Breath is the essence of life. You inhale for the very first time as you come into the world, and from that moment on you take approximately 20,000 breaths each day. Over a lifetime, you will inhale and exhale more than 500 million times. That means you have countless opportunities to utilize your breath to train your mind!

Breath meditation is known by many names, including mindfulness meditation, insight, *dharana*, zazen, shamatha, and vipassana. It's a simple practice used by many around the world and can be done anywhere, anytime, both as a formal closed-eye meditation and also as an informal way to relax and anchor your attention to the present moment while you are engaged in an activity.

This particular meditation involves bringing your focus to the subtle sensations of the breath as you naturally inhale and exhale. You feel your breath coming in, and you feel it going out. During the practice, you can focus on the area of your body where you feel the breath most prominently. Paying attention to the breath allows you to be present in the here and now. There is no particular goal, no particular sensation or experience you should be attaining. Instead, this is a practice of being present to the breath and the moment.

Some breath-awareness practices (including zazen) involve counting the breaths you "feel." Although it's not required, counting the breaths can help you become more aware of the frequency of the interruptions of your wandering mind. If you like, you can experiment with it. Simply breathe and count. You can choose your own rhythm for counting. Some people count each inhale and exhale separately. In other words: *inhale*, count one; *exhale*, count two; *inhale*, count three; etc. Others define a complete inhale/exhale cycle as one: *inhale*, *exhale*, count one; *inhale*, *exhale*, count two; etc. If you are able to count to 10 without interruption, you start again at one. There is no right way, only the way you choose. If you get interrupted while counting your breaths, you simply return to counting (again, at one). Eventually you may be able to drop the counting and simply attend to your breath.

Read through the following instructions. Review them again before your practice. It's natural not to remember each and every step, but as time goes by, this practice will become second nature.

- Before you start, determine how long you'll be doing this practice. Anywhere from 5 to 20 minutes is fine, and plan for an integration period of a few minutes afterward. Stay with it the entire practice period, even if it gets a little difficult. Most importantly, don't give up.

- Keep track of the time with a clock, watch, or meditation timer. Do not set an alarm that will make you get up to shut it off; this means no kitchen timers, no alarm clocks!

- Keep external distractions to a minimum. Put a "Do Not Disturb" sign on your door, turn off your cell phone, turn off your TV, and turn off any music—even if it's titled "meditation music"! Silence will allow you to be more mindful.

- It's natural to get distracted in meditation, so don't give yourself a hard time about losing focus. Don't be concerned by how many times you drift off. This is a practice to train your attention, enhance your ability to focus it purposely, and help you sustain it on one thing at a time.

- Let go of expectations, and don't judge or monitor your experiences in meditation. Welcome everything, resist nothing. Keep refocusing on the sensation of your breath whenever you notice you've lost the awareness of it.

- Meditation is a practice for living, so how you treat yourself in meditation is important. Be kind to yourself.

Find a comfortable sitting position. (Do not lie down while you meditate, because it can turn into a nap, and that defeats the purpose: you're working at creating more attentiveness!) Your spine should be upright. If you are sitting on the floor, your hips should be a bit higher than your knees. If you are sitting on a chair, be comfortable with your feet on the floor. Your hands can rest on your lap or knees. You don't have to hold your hands in any certain position, though you are free to experiment with what feels best for you.

Scan your body to be sure you are completely relaxed in this posture before you begin. It's okay to make slight adjustments in meditation to become more comfortable, but be sure to move mindfully.

You can close your eyes or experiment with your eyes open or just slightly open.

Breathe naturally through your nose. Bring your awareness to each breath, focusing on the movement and sensations the air creates as it moves in and out of your body.

Notice the cool air on the inhalation, the warmer air on the exhalation. Feel your chest and back rise and fall on the inhalation and exhalation. Feel your belly expand and contract.

Don't try to control the breath. Allow the breath to come and go in its own natural pattern, and simply attend to the sensations of breathing.

Keep your focus on each breath. There's nothing to imagine, nothing to figure out, nothing to control, nothing to change.

For a few breaths, let your attention rest on the natural pause between your exhale and your inhale.

Bring your attention to the whole cycle of breathing. Your breathing might spontaneously get faster or slower, deeper or shallower; it may even pause for a moment. Observe the changes without controlling the breathing pattern.

Whenever you notice your attention has drifted away from your breath—to a noise, to a thought, or to some other distraction—simply refocus your attention on the breath, again and again. (If you are counting, begin again at number one.)

If you are distracted by a physical sensation, recognize it, but don't attempt to figure out why it's happening or go into a story about it. Simply attend to the sensation; when it dissipates, return your attention to your breath.

Rest your attention on the breath and its sensations for the predetermined period of time.

When the period comes to an end, keep your eyes closed for a few minutes. Become more alert to the sounds outside of you, give yourself some deeper breaths, and stretch into the space around you. Eventually, when you feel ready, slowly open your eyes all the way. Move mindfully from stillness into activity without rushing.

Living with Awareness

The ability to be attentive and mindful is essential if you want to really enjoy your life. If you aren't paying attention, this and other moments will come and go without you even noticing. If your attention is focused elsewhere—on a past experience, or on future plans—you can miss the opportunity to savor what is happening in the present. For instance, if you are eating a lovely breakfast, but your mind is on what is for dinner, you might miss enjoying this meal right in front of you because you are so busy thinking about future possibilities. If your attention is focused on something or somewhere else, the moment will come and go, sometimes without you even noticing.

You can meet distraction with mindfulness. You can train your attention so you can be more present to who and what is in front of you. You can be a better listener, be more alert to creative impulses, make more nourishing choices, and be more present to what is truly important to you. And, no, you don't have to be a monk or a nun and run away to an ashram to become more mindful. You can begin your training right here, right now, where you are.

One simple way to be more mindful and present to life is to start the day without your phone. When I ask people in my classes which of them sleeps with their phones, there are some giggles, and then about three-quarters of the people raise their hands. Sleeping with your phone makes it easy for your attention to be hijacked immediately upon awakening. Consider what you usually do when you wake up and open your eyes: I imagine that you figure out where you are and what time it is. If you don't have a watch or a clock, the phone serves to give you the time. But, as you look at your phone, do you just see the time or do you suddenly find yourself on a train of reactivity as you check your e-mail, read texts, and check social media? Suddenly, your life is not your own! So do yourself a favor, and start your day with your own mindful agenda rather than the one being pushed at you from an electronic device. Creating healthy boundaries with your phone helps you enter the day in a more responsive, less reactive way.

Finding Daily Opportunities for Mindfulness

Throughout the day, you can make any activity an opportunity to practice mindfulness. You can be completely present while you are folding laundry, taking a shower, chopping carrots, making tea, cleaning your house, or making love. When you are attentive, you can turn a simple chore or habit into a delightful moment. All that's required is to purposely approach the activity with your full, steady, nonjudgmental attention as you engage your senses.

For instance, the next time you wash your hands, stop for a moment while standing in front of the sink. Feel your body—"be" in the experience of standing. As you turn on the water, listen to the sound as it runs. Put your hands under the faucet and experience how your hands feel as the water wets your skin. Notice the texture and scent of the soap as you put it in your hand. Observe the movement of your hands and watch how the water washes over them. Feel your arms as you reach for a towel. Notice the texture of the towel and the sensation of your hands going from wet to dry. Allow yourself to be fascinated by the moment "at hand."

The next time you have a drink of water, before bringing the cup to your lips, take a moment to notice the way the water moves in the glass. Watch the light that reflects from the surface, and feel the weight and temperature of the glass in your hand. Notice the muscles in your arms, hands, and fingers engaging to help you grip, hold, and bring the glass to your mouth. As you take a sip, be aware of the sensations of the glass meeting your lips. Notice if there is any taste, the sensations on your tongue, and how the water travels and soothes your throat as you swallow. Sense the water making its way down through your body.

Another way to be mindful is when you are in line at the grocery checkout. "Give up waiting," wrote Eckhart Tolle, the author of *The Power of Now*, and that's what you can do. Instead of waiting, daydreaming, or running through a mental to-do list, focus on the sensations in your body: feel the bottoms of your feet on the floor and the micromovements of your legs and hips as you stand. Notice your breath moving in and out, and the body's response to it. Listen to the sounds around you as they arise and return to the silence. Notice the space between objects and the space around you. Relax. Be present to all of it. What a great opportunity to practice *being* instead of doing.

Create Mindfulness Cues

Another way to remember to be mindful is to turn distractions into *mindfulness cues*. For example, every time your phone rings, why not give yourself a mindful moment? Instead of grabbing it as soon as it rings, reacting to the bell like Pavlov's dogs, you can deliberately create some spaciousness between the stimulus and your response. Break the habit of mindless reactivity by simply by pausing a moment to become present before picking up your phone.

In that moment, notice your mental and physical reactions to the simple bell. Did the sound hijack your attention from what you were doing or whom you were talking to? Did it trigger a physical response as you alerted? You can use the sound of the bell to remind you to shift your awareness back into a relaxed response; when you hear it, take a slow, deep inhale, then exhale and relax. By deliberately giving yourself a moment to be present and to relax, you can, on purpose, decide how and what you pay attention to. Remember, you do have a choice!

In fact, you have a few choices: you can answer the call, or you can decide to keep doing what you were doing and let it go to voice mail. Or, you can let it ring one more time while you bring yourself more fully present to the moment, so if you do answer the phone, you can be fully present to the person calling you.

It's important to reclaim your attention from the habitual response. Give your mind and body a break from the ongoing emergency we call life. The ringing of your phone (or of someone else's) could serve as a reminder to take a mindfulness moment: relax, reengage with what you are doing, or shift your attention on purpose to the caller.

Paying attention, moment by moment, is a new way of living for some of us. It is too late to change your past, but from now on we can be more attentive to the choices available in each moment. With mindfulness, you'll likely choose the one most nourishing for you. The present moment, this one happening right now, is when your life is lived, when you can make choices, and when you can tune in to love.

Chapter 3

The Field of Love

*We live in succession, in division, in parts,
in particles. Meantime within man is the soul of the
whole; the wise silence; the universal beauty, to which
every part and particle is equally related; the eternal One.*

—RALPH WALDO EMERSON

After decades of research in an area known as "new physics"—
the physics of relativity and quantum theory—science now supports what mystics and philosophers have insisted throughout the ages: creation is made up of an interconnected field of space, vibrating light, and intelligence.

Perhaps one of the most surprising discoveries of the last century was that the visible universe—everything that is composed of protons, neutrons, and electrons bundled together into atoms—makes up less than 5 percent of the mass of the universe. The rest of the universe, approximately 95 percent of it, is made up of dark matter and dark energy. Calling it "dark" is probably a misnomer—"transparent" might be a better word. These forces repel light and gravity, yet have a powerful effect on everything else in the universe. At this point their power is literally beyond measure. This, Emerson says, is what every part and particle is related to.

What Emerson describes in the above quote as "the soul of the whole," quantum physicists understand as a nonmaterial field that underlies and unites every quality, fundamental force, and law of nature—also beyond measure.

Albert Einstein dedicated much of his life to searching for proof of this single unseen source, or force, one powerful enough to organize all the workings of nature. His unified field theory, while incomplete, posited that the universe is composed of four basic forces: gravity, electromagnetism, and weak and strong forces. These forces not only keep us alive, but also underlie what makes life worth living, like ecstasy and energy. Space and time. Awareness and attention. Attraction and love.

This field, scientists explain, is the originating source from which all things arise. It's the ultimate essence of material phenomena. Those who are into spirituality have different names for this source: Christians and Jews call it "God." Hindus call it "Brahman." Zen Buddhists describe it as the "formless field of benefaction," *sunyata*, or "emptiness." Taoists call it "the Tao," the flow of the universe that makes the seasons change and the grass grow.

Still others use "source," "awareness," "the divine," "the Creator," "infinite intelligence," "the primordial reality pervading all of creation," or "the ocean of consciousness" to describe this seamless web that weaves together the material and nonmaterial. I've been calling it "the field of love," but in truth, it exists beyond time, space, form, and name.

The Observer Effect

The quantum physicists who followed Einstein went on to prove that this unified field is made up of tiny particles whirling through mostly empty space. What you perceive to be solid and separate things—from this book and your home to your friends and family and everything around you, including your own body—are actually made up of infinitesimally small electrons and subatomic particles that arrange themselves in response to your attention. The mere act of observing these small particles alters their behavior, and even their very existence.

As Lynne McTaggart explains in her book *The Field: The Quest for the Secret Force of the Universe*, "an electron is not a precise entity, but exists as a potential, a superposition, or sum, of all probabilities, until we observe or measure it, at which point the electron freezes into a particular state."

Scientists call this the "observer effect," which holds that the very act of watching affects the phenomenon being observed. Your attention summons these particles into existence, and once you withdraw your attention from them, they dissolve back into what McTaggart calls, "the ether of all possibilities." By virtue of where and how you direct your attention, you determine which of an infinite number of possibilities is manifested in your experience.

To summarize: Everything that appears to be still is actually moving. Everything that seems to be solid is an illusion and made up of moving particles. Everything that appears to be separated in space and time is actually connected within an unseen web of waves of light that vibrate to create everything in the physical world, including your body, the clothes you are wearing, the food you eat, the mountains, the clouds, the earth—*everything*. And things only exist because you attend to them.

This is more than just a mini-physics lesson; it is a glimpse into the awesome organizing power of your attention.

The Subtle and the Powerful

As you read these words, turn your attention to the "you" who is reading. *What is this presence that is looking through your eyes? From where does this attention arise?*

If you stay with this inquiry for a moment, you may become aware of your own awareness. This is your *you-ness*. This awareness is the essence of you that has called your body home since the day you were born, and possibly even before that. It is from this field of awareness that your attention arises. And perhaps it is the same field of love from which everything is sourced.

Awareness is very subtle, although that doesn't mean that it is insignificant or weak; it means *not noticeable*. Right now, you probably aren't noticing radio waves or gravity; while they are subtle, the strength of these forces is indisputable. As quantum physics also reminds us, the subtler something is, the more power it has. Perhaps this is why the subtle realm has intrigued and enchanted not only physicists, but also astronomers, physicians, artists, poets, and mystics throughout history, with all of them seeking to grasp the wonder and truth of creation.

So much of what these explorers seek (and find) is far beyond what can be detected with your senses, yet when the natural world is seen under an electron microscope, the complex and fragile structures and textures that exist at the subtlest level of creation are revealed: the beauty and order of a snowflake, a grain of pollen, a butterfly's wing, a fly's foot, a piece of coral, an eye cell, a poppy seed. . . . And beyond the magnificent, tiny, ordered particles that make up these everyday wonders, physicists find only vast empty space with the occasional atom or quark.

The workings of this universe of which we are all an inseparable part are far more exquisite than can be seen with our unaided eyes. As Helen Keller noted, "The best and most beautiful things in the world cannot be seen nor even touched, but just felt in the heart." Awareness is like that, and your attention is, too. It can't be seen or heard, only felt.

In ordinary states of consciousness, we perceive ourselves as distinct and separate from the world around us, or, as my friend Gregg Braden describes, as "powerless beings, victims of a world where everything is separate from everything else and we have very little influence over any of it." However, you can change this reality by expanding your awareness.

Before you begin the practice of meditation, you might live in a limited way, seeing yourself as separate, controlled by your self-image and your to-do list, and relating only to those for whom you reserve your affection. Meditation allows your contracted awareness to expand, so you can experience yourself as an integral, interrelated aspect of creation.

In meditation, your mental activity becomes less chaotic; your senses become more refined; and, depending on the practice you engage in, your attention could soon transcend thought activity, the limited reality that your five senses register and that which concerns your self-image. You instead directly experience the subtle realm from which all things arise, and this expands your awareness. With this expanded awareness, you truly experience everything as interconnected, and the soul of the whole is revealed to you. You soon see that you and your individual awareness are simply an extension of this wise, beautiful, interrelated field of love.

Ramana and the "I"

Ten years after I first went to India, I visited again with my husband, Marty. He wanted to make a pilgrimage to the ashram of one of the great sages of the 20th century, Ramana Maharshi, in the city of Tiruvannamalai in South India. Like the Dalai Lama, Ramana Maharshi's appeal crossed numerous cultural and religious boundaries due to his emphasis on discovering the true nature of the Self. (Self with a capital S refers to the true Self, the love that lives through you as you. Self with a small s refers to your self-image.)

As we made our way from the guesthouse to the ashram in a motorized rickshaw, or *tuk-tuk*, we passed an array of monkeys, street dogs, and *sadhus* who lined the roadsides, napping just about anywhere. Sadhus are holy men who wear simple dress—sometimes only a loincloth—and coat their bodies with sacred ash. They take vows of poverty and worship various deities. The ashram provides them with a daily free meal, so some of them were lining up outside of the ashram gates, waiting.

We entered the ashram gates and immediately felt the silence that pervaded the grounds, broken only by the calls of the resident peacocks. We sat and meditated in the old hall where Ramana used to meet his devotees. It was a small, simple room where he spent the later years of his life, living, sleeping, and in meditation when he wasn't circumambulating nearby Mount Arunachala, which he considered sacred.

At the age of 16, Ramana had a life-changing experience. Within the span of a few critical minutes, a process of self-inquiry spontaneously arose in him and culminated in Ramana's permanent awakening to a new reality. His description of the experience is written on a plaque in one of the rooms in the ashram: "I seldom had any sickness and on that day there was nothing wrong with my health, but a sudden violent fear of death overtook me. . . . The shock of the fear of death drove my mind inwards."

He then lay down and held his breath, imitating a corpse to create a more realistic inquiry. He asked himself, "Now death has come; what does it mean? What is it that is dying? [. . .] With the death of the body am I dead? Is the body 'I'?" An answer flashed through him vividly: "*I* am Spirit transcending the body. The body dies but the spirit that transcends it cannot be touched by death. This means *I* am the deathless Spirit." (Italics mine.)

From that moment onward he reported that the "I" focused its attention on itself with a powerful fascination. His individual self and its ego became lost in the flood of Self-awareness. This absorption in the Self continued unbroken throughout his life. Even though thoughts came and went, the "I" was ever-present.

After this experience, he left his family home to dwell in a cave on the side of one of India's holiest mountains, Arunachala, and eventually became a sought-after spiritual teacher.

Ramana was reported to radiate a powerful silence that quieted the minds of those who sought his counsel. When any aspirant asked for his advice, he'd respond with a question, such as "From where did that thought arise?" His questions were invitations to his students to inquire deeply into their own natures, to ultimately answer the question "Who am I?" for themselves, just as he had done.

Questions such as "Who am I?" and "Where did that thought arise from?" are much like the Japanese Zen Buddhist *koans*, a form of inquiry that bypasses what I refer to as the "I know" mind. Koans are questions designed to promote a direct experience of life, rather than a philosophical discourse. They function as a kind of unlearning, as the questions themselves demand transcending the intellect to directly experience the Self. Ramana believed inquiry was the fastest track to enlightenment, though he said it wasn't a fit for everybody. The other track, he said, is surrender.

Whether you choose the path of surrendering to the love that moves through you, or the path of inquiring into the nature of your own being, you'll discover that there is love: unconditional, infinite, and ever-present. What Ramana calls the "I" is this current of love that lives through you as you, and lives through me as me. It isn't limited by birth or death or the transient activities of the body or mind or life.

The "I" is what is looking through your eyes. It is what is paying attention. It arises in you, as you, from that limitless and powerful field of existence. It does not differentiate or discriminate; it has no condition. Instead, it simply *is*, the same way that the sun simply shines on everything without an agenda. It gives and receives. It is natural, unlimited, and available everywhere at all times. It is love and love is ever-present and everlasting. You only have to wake up to it and, as the Dalai Lama says, "the true nature of things and events."

Mantras: Whisper Words of Wisdom

I've experienced, or at least experimented with, just about every type of meditation, but for years my go-to practice has been a silent, mantra-based meditation. It facilitates what is known as transcendence—which means, literally, to "go beyond."

I was first taught a mantra in the United States when I learned Transcendental Meditation. It was the same technique that the Beatles had learned when they traveled to India to study with

Maharishi Mahesh Yogi. I learned it from a sweet American man wearing a leisure suit in a brownstone in Washington, D.C. I'd met with him for an introductory lecture and returned a day later for my mantra, bringing flowers, a piece of fruit, and a new white handkerchief, as he had instructed. He took me upstairs to a meditation room smelling sweetly of incense.

He asked me to stand and watch him perform a ceremony, during which he chanted mantras that honored his tradition and the teachers before him. This, he said, prepared me to receive the mantra. I sat in the chair in front of him and he whispered my mantra gently into my ear, then had me whisper it, then silently repeat it. I successfully meditated for a 20-minute period, and I fell in love with the practice.

It doesn't matter whether you receive your mantra in a ceremony or you find one you like within these pages. Mantras are effective, regardless of the source. (I've included more detail about specific mantras later in this chapter.)

Mantras work to settle the mind in meditation because the repetition of the sound of the mantra itself serves to interrupt the constant monologue of thoughts and daydreams. Some people chant mantras all day long, as in a prayer practice, to keep their focus on various aspects of the divine. However, in this book, we concern ourselves simply with the use of mantras in meditation.

It's said we have anywhere from 12,000 to 70,000 thoughts a day, consisting of words or images strung together in the mind. The meaning of each thought leads to another, and on and on. When you interrupt thoughts by repeating a sound without meaning (such as a mantra), your mental activity naturally begins to settle down, and thoughts themselves become subtler and subtler. Soon, you are no longer concerned with thoughts.

As your thoughts become mostly meaningless noise, you lose track of the transitory aspects of yourself. You lose track of your environment—where you are or who is nearby. You lose track of your body; for instance, you might not be able to feel your hands or feet. Your self-image is no longer so important, and your personal issues fade to the background. Soon, your attention is no longer engaged with the objects you usually concern yourself with. Instead of being aware of any *thing* in particular, you dive into that field of undifferentiated awareness. You transcend everything but awareness itself.

It is your gentle attention on a mantra which takes you on a deep dive into that awareness which is looking through your eyes. It's not that you are checked out; instead, you are checked in. Your attention checks in and meets the field from which all of creation arises. It's awareness meeting awareness.

Transcendence

Transcendence is a natural by-product of gently directing your natural attention on a focal point in meditation. It is something that occurs spontaneously; you can't make it happen with sheer willpower. Though it can and does happen while you are living your regular life, it is not common. Transcendence seems to be more easily encouraged through meditation, most often while using a mantra.

In meditation, the state of transcendence allows the direct experience of pure awareness, the field of love. This field is subtle and intangible. As an illustration of this, consider the way that both gravity and electricity are subtle forces with no real dimension, and yet they are obviously powerful. You can't point to either of these forces or sense them in their pure forms, but you can certainly experience their effects.

The same is true of pure awareness. As you transcend the relative world of time and space and slip into this field of love, you won't have a sensory experience. You won't "experience" it as you would things with dimension in time and space, because this field has no dimension. Instead, you commune with it; you unite with it. Transcendence is a state—a union with the field of love—and it is impossible to identify while it's happening. This phenomenon has been described as "being in the gap," or slipping into the space between your thoughts, where the thinker resides.

Transcendence is a moment when you no longer experience separation between yourself and any other thing. You are still aware, but not engaged with linear reality in the sense that you no longer experience where you begin and end. Duality disappears as you, the subject, and everything else, the objects, merge into pure awareness itself. This union is the direct experience of your true Self *existing as the field of love.*

You only realize the phenomenon after moments go by, and then your thoughts arise. *Where am I? I could meditate forever, it feels so great!* Some people report a feeling of expansion and bliss after it occurs. But when you become aware of what you are feeling, the subject-object split has recurred: there is you, and there are your thoughts, so you are no longer transcending. Much like the observer effect alters the state and existence of particles, the moment you recognize that you are transcending is also a recognition that you are no longer in a transcendental state.

Robert Adams, the late American mystic, described transcendence as melding into silence:

> True silence really means going deep within yourself to that place where nothing is happening, where you transcend time and space. You go into a brand new dimension of nothingness. That's where all the power is. That's your real home. That's where you really belong, in deep silence where there is no good or bad, no one trying to achieve anything. Just being, pure being. . . . Silence is the ultimate reality.

The state of transcendence is powerful, sometimes even overwhelming. It is a moment during which your individual sense of self merges and becomes one with something much more expansive. Though meditation can cultivate and encourage transcendence, it is not something you can force or will into being. Recurring transcendence can lead to the ability to see the world in a new, awakened way and is a natural and completely spontaneous perspective.

Jill Bolte Taylor, a Harvard-trained neurobiologist, had a unique opportunity to explore the nature of her own being while suffering a stroke. She was able to stay cognizant throughout much of the ordeal and watched the stroke's effects on her perception of reality as the left side of her brain lost function. This experience changed the way she saw herself, the world, and her place in it. The stroke gave her the direct experience of knowing that she is part of the whole. In a TED Talk, she shared her experience:

> I look down at my arm and I realize that I can no longer define the boundaries of my body. I can't define where I begin and where I end, because the atoms and the molecules of my arm blended with the atoms and molecules of the wall, and all that I could detect is this energy—energy.
>
> And I'm asking myself, "What is wrong with me? What is going on?" And in that moment my left hemisphere brain chatter went totally silent. . . . I was shocked to find myself inside a silent mind. Then I was immediately captivated by the magnificence of the energy around me . . . I felt enormous and expansive. I felt at one with all the energy that was, and it was beautiful there.

I think grace has something to do with transcendence; it often occurs in moments when you're not expecting anything in particular, but are simply open to receiving.

When transcendence does occur, you can't hold on to the experience because it isn't a thing. You can't go "there," because it isn't a place either. It has no location in space or time.

Trying to Transcend

It's not possible for you to *make* yourself transcend. Once you've felt the sweetness and expansion that result from transcending, you may have the strong desire to do so over and over again. It's important to remember, however, that transcending in meditation has nothing to do with willpower or skillful thinking. You cannot decide it will happen, or think your way there. *Trying* to achieve it is not helpful either.

How often you transcend, and the length of time it spans, really seems to depend on your nervous system. How much stress you've been under or have accumulated over your lifetime, what you ate recently, how you've been sleeping, your emotional state, your habits, and so on certainly can have an effect on the settling down of the nervous system in meditation.

As Yoda from the Star Wars series says, "Do or do not. There is no try." I encourage you to approach each meditation with a beginner's mind—welcoming everything and expecting nothing—and practice with ease and see what happens.

Transcendence can occur in meditation, and it can happen with your eyes open, too. You don't have to be on a mountaintop, travel to India, or have a brain injury to transcend. There's no need to follow a religious doctrine, nor do you have to pretend to be spiritual or do endless acts of charity. It doesn't require any special powers of concentration; it doesn't even require thinking.

Enlightened teachers that I've studied with say that all that is needed to consciously connect with the field of love is the deep desire to know it. The field reveals itself to those who patiently seek it with an open mind and heart. All the obstacles that have come between you and your experience of it—distracting habits of mind, overidentification with your self-image, feeling separate, unconscious repressed and suppressed beliefs, self-defeating thoughts, and overobjectifying reality—are revealed so as to be eliminated, and then your awareness expands.

If it is your desire, the day will come for you to surrender to the expansion, as described by writer Anais Nin: "the risk to remain tight in a bud was more painful than the risk it took to blossom." Meanwhile, it's important to live with mindful awareness so that you are attentive enough to surrender to the field when it calls you.

Fusion with the Field of Love

As you continue your daily meditation practice, you build and energize your connection to the inner dimensions of life. It's like diving into a pool full of water with the qualities of peace, power, silence, equanimity, potential, timelessness, boundlessness, perfection, purity, and love. Once you come out of the pool, you are "wet" with the water and its qualities. The awareness of the field of love can seep into your life and create a new way of seeing reality, even when you are not in meditation.

In J. D. Salinger's short story "Teddy," a spiritually curious boy recalls awakening to the oneness of all things while watching his little sister drink a glass of milk. "All of a sudden I saw that *she* was God and the *milk* was God. I mean, all she was doing was pouring God into God."

Such moments of awakening are not uncommon, and when they occur, life as we know it is transformed—sometimes dramatically. A recent study at the University of Chicago reports that nearly half of all Americans have had a peak experience, where reality as they had once known it has changed. You may have had a few yourself. If the experience lasted only a second or two, you might simply have dismissed it as a nice feeling that punctuated an otherwise ordinary, three-dimensional life.

Perhaps you are one who recognizes the moment's significance, whether the insight lasted a few seconds, a few days, or even a few months. You might realize that you've had a glimpse into the fabric of the usually unseen realm of life: one that you've always sensed the existence of. Intuitively, you understand that this is the beauty and wonder from which your soul is born. This is the field from which creation arises in all its glory.

The moments are sometimes the impetus to embark on a spiritual path in pursuit of what Thomas Aquinas called "the experiential knowledge of God." Mystics over the ages have reported that some of these moments are accompanied by ineffable visions, melodic voices, heavenly music, and ecstatic rapture that go way beyond the realms of ordinary life.

Hasidic Jews describe the awakening to this love as *being absorbed within God's Infinite Light*. "Let the light penetrate the darkness until the darkness itself shines and there is no longer any division between the two," reads one passage from *Tales of the Hasidim* by Martin Buber.

Zen Buddhists call the moment of awakening *satori* or *kensho*. Taoism describes it as knowing the Tao or "the Way." Quakers refer to it as "seeing the light" in everyone, while yogis use the word *samadhi* to describe transcending the relative world and experiencing the fusion of knower and known.

With meditation, and by dwelling in this field, you will awaken to realize that everything is part of you; nothing is separate from you. There is fusion, where the subject and the object, the lover and the beloved, merge. And as all fusion does, it creates light. Enlightenment.

About Mantras

There are many mantras that you can use in meditation to facilitate transcendence and fusion with the field of love. Mantras are found in every culture and religion, and the word itself comes from the combination of two syllables: *man* meaning "mind," and *tra*, meaning "vehicle." A mantra is a sound, word, or phrase that is repeated over and over, whether you say it aloud, chant it silently to yourself, or even write it. Using a mantra can facilitate a journey from the external world into the space between your thoughts, into the space from which your thoughts arise, to your centerpoint of peace.

I'm most familiar with and teach the Sanskrit mono- and bi-syllabic mantras used in meditation. They're called *bija* or "seed" mantras and are considered primordial sounds that are linguistic representations of the elemental sounds of nature. Bija mantras are considered laser beams of sound that, when repeated, allow for transcendence and expanded awareness. Some even work on various energy centers of the body, enhancing vitality and purifying toxicity.

The most common bija mantra is *Om* or *Aum* (also said to be the root for the word "amen," or *ameen* in Hebrew and Arabic). It's a word that can be said alone, or before any other mantra to empower it. I enjoy using and teaching the mantra *Ma Om*. This mantra is repeated in conjunction with the breath. You silently think *Ma*, a sound that enlivens the divine creative feminine energy, on the inhale. Then, on the exhale, you silently think *Om*, which invokes divine light (i.e., pure potential). In meditation, the silent repetition of these sounds invokes both pure potential and infinite creativity. Try it now for a minute and see how powerful these simple bija mantras can be.

Various ancient languages—among them Hebrew, Aramaic, Sanskrit, Pali, Tamil, Latin, and Arabic—give rise to mantras. This is because the sounds of the words in these languages more closely reflect what they represent than do the sounds of those words in the more modern Romance languages.

In the Christian tradition, for example, the mantra *Maranatha*, a word in ancient Aramaic that means "Come, O Lord," is traditionally used in centering prayer. Others repeat the phrase *Kyrie eleison*, which means "Lord, have mercy." Those in the Jewish tradition might repeat the phrase *Ribono Shel Olam*, which means "Lord of the universe," a phrase used for centuries by Hasidic mystics. Some repeat *Neshama*, which means "soul, spirit, or divine spark."

The *Om Mane Padme Hum* mantra of Tibetan Buddhism is repeated while walking or bowing. It is translated as "the jewel in the lotus of the heart," a reference to the hidden spark of divinity within each one of us that can blossom eternally. The lotus is a symbol found in many Eastern religions that is analogous to the spiritual journey many of us take from darkness to light. Each one of us inherently has the ability to open our awareness to the divine, whether you see it clearly now or not.

In Islam, *Allahu akbar*—"God is great"—remains one of the more popular mantras. Others are *Bismillah ir-Rahman ir-Rahim*, which means "in the name of God, the merciful, the compassionate." Popular too is the simple repetition of *Allah, Allah*. In ancient Egypt, a popular mantra was *Ankh ba*, translated as "the soul lives."

There are also devotional mantras that call on one specific deity or saint. Catholics chant *Hail Mary* or *Ave Maria* as they mark each repetition with a bead on their rosary. There are Hindu mantras: *Om Gam Ganapataye Namaha* translates as "salutations to Lord Ganesha" (the elephant-headed god responsible for removing obstacles); *Om Hreem Sri Laksmi Namaha* calls to the goddess Laxmi to bestow material and spiritual abundance; and *Om Namah Shivaya* honors Shiva, which in this context means devotion to your true identity, or consciousness itself.

In Sanskrit, the word for divine love is *Prema*, which is the highest, most expanded form of love, the love of God. (The meaning is similar to the Greek *agape*.) You can incorporate it into a mantra practice by repeating *Aham* (which means "I am") and *Prema* ("divine love").

There are longer Sanskrit chants, such as the 100-syllable purification prayer of the Tibetan Buddhists, the Vajrasattva mantra. There are also the Rig Veda and the Sama Veda (ancient Vedic chants dating back to 5000 B.C.E. and still recited today in India). The Gayatri mantra, a Vedic chant and one of my favorites, is chanted for all beings to reach enlightenment. You can listen online to a lovely version of it sung by Deva Premal on YouTube. I listen to and sing along with it most mornings.

The mantras given out in Transcendental Meditation (TM) are allotted based on a simple formula: the age and sex of the meditator. There are about 20 TM mantras, called Shakti mantras, that are said to invoke the divine feminine, represented in this case by the great Hindu goddesses. Some of these mantras are *Aim*, *Hrim*, *Kirim*, and *Shrim*, pronounced Ah-YEEM, Hir-EEM, Kir-EEM, and Shir-EEM, respectively. (For the correct pronunciations, you can listen to a guide on YouTube.)

Most mantras can be spelled in a variety of ways, and though they might be interesting to read, the real benefit of using one can only be experienced, not explained or intellectualized. I believe these mantras are to be used with deep respect, as they can invoke powerful creative forces that emerge from the essential field of love.

Getting Your Mantra On

One way to find a mantra is to receive it from a teacher, or a guru. There are popular magazines that suggest that you can choose your own mantra from any pleasant word, such as *joy*, *peace*, or *love*. Some people have told me that they wait for a mantra to choose them.

In general, mantras used in meditation are to be used for their sound quality, rather than their meaning. Every word, whether it's *table* or *mountain*, has two components: its sound (in Sanskrit, *shruti*, or "that which is heard")—TAY-bul or MOWN-tan—and a meaning that we all agree on (in Sanskrit, *smriti*.) That's what language is, an agreement that certain sounds mean certain things. For the most part, those two components are inseparable, but they can certainly be separated. Have you ever had the experience of repeating a word aloud over and over again, and, somehow, it became disconnected from its meaning? That's a separation between sound and meaning.

Many of the mantras discussed in this book have some meaning, and there are specific mantras that should definitely be reserved for use in a formal meditation practice. Bija mantras, for example, are repeated while focusing on the sound of the mantra itself, not on the meaning or any memory or association that the sound may trigger within you. Remember, it's the sound of the mantra itself that interrupts thought and settles the mind.

Mantra Meditation Practice

The mantra we'll use for this practice is *HamSah*, pronounced "hahm sah" (the *m* is soft, almost like the sound *ng*). This mantra is loosely translated as "I am that," and has been used for thousands of years. This is a bija mantra, so linguistically it represents the subtlest sounds of the breath. (Another version of this mantra is *So Hum*.)

Remember, when you use one of these or any other mantra, it's ideal to focus on the sound rather than the meaning of the word.

The following is a formal practice. This means you'll use this mantra in meditation rather than throughout your day. However, if for some reason the mantra comes to your mind while you are in activity, return your focus to the activity you are engaged in. If you get distracted by some mental or physical activity while in meditation, return your focus to the mantra.

Read through the following instructions, and review them again the first few times you practice. It's natural not to remember each and every step, but as time goes by, this practice will become second nature. Ideally, practice meditation every day, twice a day.

- Determine how long you'll be doing this practice before you start: choose a period of time from 5 to 30 minutes. Stick to your plan no matter how good or bad you deem the experiences. Include a few minutes at the end for an integration period.

- Keep track of the time with a clock, watch, or meditation timer. Do not set an alarm that you will have to get up to shut off: no kitchen timers, no alarm clocks!

- Keep distractions to a minimum—put a "Do Not Disturb" sign on your door, turn off your cell phone, turn off your TV, and turn off music. Silence will allow you to turn your attention inward.

- Do not lie down while you meditate. Find a comfortable position sitting up. Your spine should be upright and your hips should be higher than your knees. Rest your hands on your lap, or on your knees, palms up or palms down. You don't have to hold them in any certain position, though you are free to experiment with what feels best for you.

- It's okay to make slight adjustments in your position during meditation to create more comfort—but be sure to move mindfully.

- It's okay to have thoughts in meditation. They have nothing to do with how deep you are going or whether you are doing it correctly. As you sit, all kinds of thoughts will arise. They come and go every few seconds. Thoughts can be in words, such as thinking about desires, goals, and everyday activities. Thoughts can be visual, too: memories, colors, shapes, faces, and places. It doesn't matter how many times you lose the mantra; your job is simply to notice when you are off topic, and then return your attention to the mantra again and again. This is the training of your attention.

- Let go of expectations, don't try too hard, and be gentle with yourself. Welcome everything, resist nothing. Stay with the entire practice period and don't give up.

Close your eyes.

Give yourself three long, slow, deep breaths through your nose. Then, allow your breath to settle to its natural rhythm and depth.

Feel your body as you sit still. Scan it to relax from the top of your head, face, shoulders, arms, back, chest, belly, hips, and legs. Don't resist sensations; simply become aware of them.

Notice and welcome the different sounds that become apparent to you. Notice how most will arise from the silence and return to the silence, just like the sound of your breath.

Bring your attention to the sensations of your breath as you breathe naturally through your nose. Notice the movement of the body in response to the breath. Do not control or regulate the breath; simply feel for a few minutes.

After a few minutes, on an inhale, think the sound "hahm." As you exhale, think the sound "sah." (If you prefer a different sound or mantra, adapt these instructions for that practice.)

Gently repeat the mantra like this for a few breaths.

On an inhalation, gently draw your breath along the back of your throat and listen for the sound of "hahm" in your actual breath. As you exhale, listen for the sound of "sah" as your breath is amplified in the throat. Continue in this way for a few breaths.

Relax your throat and continue to silently repeat the mantra. Let your mind become absorbed in the sound of HamSah in your internal chanting. There's nothing to figure out, no particular feeling you should feel.

Whenever you notice that your attention has drifted away from your mantra to a sound in the environment, a sensation, or a thought, gently refocus on the mantra. There is no need to force, enunciate, or concentrate.

In meditation, all kinds of thoughts will arise. They come and go every few seconds. Don't try to stop them, but when you notice they have carried your attention away, gently reintroduce the mantra with your breath again. Allow the mantra to again become the focus. This is the training of your attention. Be kind to yourself.

If you notice you are distracted by a physical sensation, bring your attention to it and feel it without judgment until it dissipates. Don't tell yourself a story. Instead, simply be aware of the sensation. Remember, your nonjudgmental attention is love. When other thoughts arise and you are no longer feeling the sensation, return to the mantra.

If you notice a particular emotion, sense where you feel it in your body. Don't analyze where it came from or why you are having it. Instead, feel it—let the emotion have its life. Then return to the mantra.

Continue meditating this way for the entire period.

When the period ends, it's very important to allow yourself a few minutes for integration before jumping back into activity. Keep your eyes closed, stop saying the mantra, and sit easily for at least 1 or 2 minutes. During this integration period, you can gently stretch your body, say a prayer or affirmation, or just bathe in the silence of your own being. After a few minutes, slowly open your eyes.

Keeping Up Your Practice

The moment you recognize you are distracted by thoughts in meditation is a *choice point*; it's a term in physics that indicates an opportunity for branching or forking toward a variety of possibilities. In meditation, this is when you have the choice to either return your attention back to the focus of your meditation or continue your daydream. Each time you keep your commitment to refocus, you train your brain. When you practice making the most nourishing choice (to keep on meditating), you develop your ability to make nourishing choices both in meditation and in your life.

It is the nature of the mind to think, so thoughts will arise naturally and spontaneously in meditation. Often, the thoughts are a narrative of what is happening in your life or what is happening in meditation. They can include what has happened or what will happen. If you have a thought that you feel is important, it will be there when you come out of meditation. However, most thoughts are mundane and will be forgotten afterward.

It's important to stick with your time commitment until the time period is up. Keep coming back to your focus as soon as you realize your attention has drifted away from it, even if you have to do so over and over again. When you make a commitment to sit through these rough spots, you'll feel really refreshed afterward. You'll also change your relationship to that reactive part of your brain and become more responsive rather than reactive. Committing to a time keeps the mind a little more settled, and trains the attention to focus and the body to settle down into a relaxed state.

Stress Release in Meditation

Though many think meditation should be peaceful (and sometimes it is), it's also an opportunity for stress release. Meditation is called the ideal antidote to stress because it allows the body and mind to release the stress that inhibits optimal function and balance.

Deepak Chopra has said that if you are restless and bored, it's a good meditation. This is because these experiences often indicate that your body is releasing stress. So if you are having a restless meditation, stay with the practice. You may or may not experience a meditator's high after the stress is released, but either way, you'll definitely feel better when you've completed the meditation.

The stress released in meditation can come from a variety of sources, such as emotional experiences, environmental influences, and physical issues. Stress is also caused by not being fully present to the experience of your life, and from not saying what you mean or doing what you say. It can come from traumatic events, from difficult relationships, and from not taking care of yourself. All stressors, including the experiences you didn't fully "digest," leave a subtle residue in the mind and body. This is what begins to accumulate and inhibits your mind-body connection. It contracts your awareness and veils your connection to who you really are.

As the body and mind settle down in meditation, stress has the opportunity to be released. This allows the body's energy and intelligence to flow more freely, enlivening the mind-body connection. This release happens naturally, and, as it does, it creates correlating movements. These movements can come as a surprise, and they are not always physical. They can include:

- Movement of the mind (including ideas, thoughts, visuals, colors)

- Surfacing of emotions (releases such as crying, smiling, and fleeting sensations of joy, anxiety, or anger)

- Movement of the body (including tingling, twitching, pain, temperature changes, itching, and vibrations)

Stress Release and Mental Activity

Thoughts in meditation are often an indication of stress being released; however, the content of your thoughts usually doesn't have anything to do with the source of the stress being released. For instance, you might be thinking of a work issue during meditation, but you could be releasing some stress from a long-ago experience.

Colors that you see in meditation are also related to the release of stress. Sometimes the colors you see correlate to the body's energy centers (chakras). The release of subtle stress allows the energy channels to open, and they become enlivened.

If you are releasing a lot of stress, you may have so many internal distractions that you don't feel like you are having a deep meditation. Yet if you were able to check your body's vital signs (such as blood pressure, heart rate, and respiration rate), you'd probably discover you are deeply resting. The reality is that your body can be in a deep, calm state even if your mind is active.

In meditation, your job is simple: don't get too enamored with following your thoughts. Instead, notice when your attention isn't on the mantra, and simply return to the focus, time and time again.

Stress Release and Emotions

In meditation, the deep relaxation you attain allows a kind of unwinding or purification to occur. Emotions that have been under the surface get released. Strong emotions such as fear, grief, sadness, anger, anxiety, or compassion can arise.

You might wonder where all these emotions are coming from. If you are uncomfortable with a particular emotion, it may be arising because you ignored it when it showed up in your everyday life. Perhaps you repressed it or thought you could wait to feel it at another, more convenient time; but, of course, it's not possible to schedule emotions. The truth is, emotions arise and should be paid attention to in real time. Emotions are "energy in motion." If you habitually resist their natural energetic flow and don't fully attend to them when they come, the energy of the emotion becomes "stuck" in your nervous system.

When an emotion does arise in meditation, you might be tempted to interpret why it arose, or dramatize its existence with a story. For example, if anger arises, you might immediately want to connect it to some past incident or to something in the present moment, such as a noise in the room or pain in your body.

If you truly bear witness to an emotion as it arises, you'll notice that it comes in its pure state—arising as pure feeling without associated thoughts. So it's best not to interpret or analyze the reason for the emotion, as this mental gyration can intensify or distract you from the pure emotion. Let go of the story lines, but don't ignore the feeling that arises. Instead, identify where in the body you feel it, and pay attention to it so the energy of the emotion can move through. Once the feeling dissipates, return to the focus of your meditation.

Stress Release and Physical Sensations

During meditation, strong physical sensations such as tingling, pain, coughing, twitching, tearing up, jerking, or swallowing excessively can indicate stress release. The area where you experience the sensation is usually the area from which the stress is being released, or has just been released, and now the area is rebalancing.

If your whole body moves or sways, or if you feel temperature changes, heaviness, or lightness, these sensations can indicate a shift in the subtler aspects of your body, such as its energy system or your hormones.

Physical sensations in meditation can also be a choice point with several healthy options. You could bear witness to how your body feels, without a narrative and without attempting to change your experience; then, once the sensation dissipates, return your attention to the focus of your meditation. Alternatively, you could choose to move mindfully to get more comfortable. Finally, you could simply ignore the sensation and refocus on your breath or mantra.

Stress Release and Correlations

A student once asked me why the random thoughts we often experience in meditation don't have much to do with what stress is being released, yet the physical and emotional content do correlate. I explained to her that it's the movement of the mind that creates content; the mind tells us stories constantly. The body's structure and subtle energy channels, on the other hand, are content-free. Thus, the movements relating to stress moving out of the body are expressed and experienced as physical sensations rather than stories.

In other words, physical movements are purely sensation. The body doesn't make stories up, so if you are releasing pain or normalizing hormones, the body will do just that without a story. It twitches, it moves, it breathes. The mind, however, likes to interfere and tell stories about why this or that happened and what you should do about it. That's why the movement of the mind is simply an indication of stress being released, and the generated movement (thought) is generally not related to the stress itself.

The mind thinks, labels, categorizes, judges, and travels, and it's common for most of us become charmed by our thoughts. Remember, you don't have to believe everything you think, just because you think it. Don't let thoughts and your "I know" mind sidetrack you, especially on your voyage into the world of expanded awareness through meditation.

Glimpsing the Soul

Each of us lives with three states of consciousness: waking, dreaming, and sleeping. Each of these states has differentiated physiological markers (respiration rates, blood pressure, and brain activity) and differentiated levels of awareness (dull, active, alert).

When you are awake, you're aware of thoughts, experiences, and feelings. Your brain waves are generally in beta or alpha states, and you are actively aware. Just before sleep, there is a floating sensation between being awake and falling asleep. This is when your brain is settling down. Your brain waves will be in an alpha state, then settle into a deeper theta state while you are dreaming.

Your dreamless sleep is reflected in the delta waves; this is when there is no awareness of emotions, thoughts, or images, and you are disconnected from your senses, environment, and experiences. This is a dull level of awareness; you are certainly much less aware than while you are awake or dreaming.

In meditation, you have access to a state of consciousness that differs from these—a transcendent state: the fourth state of consciousness. In Sanskrit, this is called *atma darshan*, or *turiya*, which means directly experiencing your own soul. It's also called *soul consciousness*, or *transcendental consciousness*. This naturally occurs in meditation as you become deeply relaxed, and your mind settles down. Your breath might even stop.

In transcendence, you are no longer aware of the focus of your meditation; there might be no mental activity or thought forms at all. Instead of being aware of anything, there is simply awareness as you (the subject) and that which you pay attention to (the object) merge. Transcendence can seem a little dreamlike or like sleep, but it isn't a dream at all. Instead, you'll be deeply relaxed yet completely awake. It is the direct experience of bliss and deep peace. It's a state of restful alertness.

Remember, you can't will transcendence into happening; it is a natural result of the effortless meditation process, just as sleeping and dreaming are natural processes of life. With a regular practice of meditation, you will have the direct experience of the vast undifferentiated field of awareness. The awareness of it will begin to wake up inside of you while you are living your life in the three other states.

Gradually, a "new normal" will develop. Instead of being rocked by the ever-changing landscape of the external world and its good and bad news, and your reactions to it, you will find a more stable state of effortless being. You will take things less personally and come to see everything that exists simply as a play of consciousness, of which you are a part.

You will awaken to a new reality, one where you are connected with everything through a web of existence. You become aware of the field of awareness. This is the field—the silent source from which your attention arises—which will illuminate all the barriers you've erected against knowing it intimately.

Chapter 4

Awakening to Love

Your task is not to seek for love, but merely to seek and find all the barriers within yourself that you have built against it.

—RUMI

Poets, philosophers, and mystics throughout the ages have contemplated the mystery of love, and yet it still defies description. Each of us can feel the effects of love, but we don't quite know *what* it is because it has no true form, no true face.

From the perspectives of biology, anthropology, sociology, and even neuroscience, the most practical way to define love is as a verb. "To love" is to create a union between subject and object. The subject is you, and whether you fall in love with another person, an idea, a cause, nature, God, or your work, you will be so charmed by this object that you'll follow the path that love shows you, all the way home to unite with the field of love as expressed through you and as the object of your love.

Love is the merging of subject and object. It is a fusion. This is also what happens when you transcend in meditation as your attention merges with its source: the field of love. The space between you and that which you focus your natural attention on dissolves. Two become one, and this fusion creates light.

This awakening to love requires lifting the veil of ignorance, conditions, and concerns that have separated you from knowing yourself as love. Egoic, self-limiting beliefs such as *I'm not lovable, I'm not good enough,* and *There's something wrong with me* can prevent you from connecting and being present for another. They can prevent you from experiencing the love that you are and the love that surrounds you. Fortunately, as your awareness expands, your habitual thoughts and limiting beliefs are illuminated. Once met, acknowledged, and questioned in the light of love, they will fall away, dissolved by the truth that separation is an illusion.

Your ego may experience this expansion as a threat without your old friends of self-doubt and separation. You might be frightened and tempted to return to what is familiar. But what the ego deems to be loss of control is instead the dissolution of old habits, grudges, judgments, prejudices, and limitations that had prevented you from opening to love. The expansion awakens you to love, and ultimately love wins.

Be Love Now

Love expands your heart and encompasses everything, great and small. When you awaken to love—and I am not referring to romantic love alone but when you are *being* love—love radiates to everything: every living being you meet, all things near and far, every pebble on the trail, every star in the sky, and all that ever existed or will exist.

One of my favorite spiritual teachers, Ram Dass, profoundly contributed to the Western world's understanding of consciousness and the potential that we each have to awaken to it. When I was 10 years old, my best friend's mother brought his first book, *Be Here Now,* to the beach one summer. As a child, I was immediately intrigued by his way of seeing the world.

Ram Dass was born in 1931 by the name of Richard Alpert. After earning his bachelor's degree from Tufts, a master's from Wesleyan, and a doctorate in psychology from Stanford, he became a professor at Harvard. He first explored transcendence while conducting experiments at Harvard with his colleague,

Timothy Leary. They were researching the therapeutic use of hallucinogenic drugs, which eventually led to their dismissal from the university. Subsequently, Ram Dass left to travel through India. There, he met a Hindu guru called Neem Karoli Baba, whom he credits with transforming his life.

In a later book, *Be Love Now,* Ram Dass describes the meeting during which he awakened to love:

> If I go into the place in myself that is love and you go into the place in yourself that is love, we are together in love. Then you and I are truly in love, the state of being love. That's the entrance to Oneness. That's the space I entered when I met my guru.
>
> Years ago in India I was sitting in the courtyard of the little temple in the Himalayan foothills. Thirty or forty of us were there around my guru, Maharaj-ji. This old man wrapped in a plaid blanket was sitting on a plank bed, and for a brief uncommon interval everyone had fallen silent. It was a meditative quiet, like an open field on a windless day or a deep clear lake without a ripple. I felt waves of love radiating toward me, washing over me like a gentle surf on a tropical shore, immersing me, rocking me, caressing my soul, infinitely accepting and open.
>
> I was nearly overcome, on the verge of tears, so grateful and so full of joy it was hard to believe it was happening. I opened my eyes and looked around, and I could feel that everyone else around me was experiencing the same thing. I looked over at my guru. He was just sitting there, looking around, not doing anything. It was just his being, shining like the sun equally on everyone. It wasn't directed at anyone in particular. For him it was nothing special, just his own nature.
>
> This love is like sunshine, a natural force, a completion of what is, a bliss that permeates every particle of existence. In Sanskrit it's called *sat-cit-ananda*, "truth-consciousness-bliss," the bliss of consciousness of

existence. That vibrational field of *ananda* love permeates everything; everything in that vibration is in love. It's a different state of being beyond the mind. We were transported by Maharaj-ji's love from one vibrational level to another, from the ego to the soul level. When Maharaj-ji brought me to my soul through that love, my mind just stopped working. Perhaps that's why unconditional love is so hard to describe, and why the best descriptions come from mystic poets. Most of our descriptions are from the point of view of conditional love, from an interpersonal standpoint that just dissolves in that unconditioned place.

After returning to America, Ram Dass continued to teach and write. Then, in 1997, he had an experience that he calls grace, though many probably wouldn't: he suffered a stroke. In a recent teleconference, his ability to speak was noticeably hindered by paralysis from the stroke, but his message was very clear. He insisted that when we acknowledge and meet people where they are, without an agenda, *this is love.* He knows that one's natural, gentle, unencumbered attention is love.

The Love School

Love's deepest desire is to awaken you to the fullness of who you are, and all that you are here to experience, share, and create. This love in you can shine like the sun, and on everyone and everything. Truly, this is all love seeks. Your life experiences, your heartbreaks, your challenges, your joys—all are the curriculum that calls you home to realize the field of love.

Someone once said, "What you are seeking is seeking you." I've also heard, "What you are looking for, is what is looking." This "what" is love—it's that pure awareness looking through your eyes.

Love is truthful, generous, healing, reverent, contented, pure, free, compassionate, benevolent, present, patient, wise, blissful, abundant, eternal, infinite, and powerful. By its very nature, love is unconditioned and unconditional. You could even say that the term *unconditional love* is redundant.

In actuality, there is no such thing as conditional love. If there are conditions, it cannot be love; it is something else. It can be a relationship labeled as "love," where the space between you and who or what you love is glazed with conditions such as neediness, lust, attachment, dependence, expectation, judgment, or greed. It is based on what the other will do for you, what the other will give you, or how the other can make you feel. With each party focused on what they are getting from it, the relationship is transactional rather than relational. It serves the ego and self-image rather than the heart.

When we view people, places, things, and even ourselves through the lens of the preferences, labels, expectations, and beliefs we've constructed, then our ability to consciously live in this field of love, and to give and receive it fully, is limited.

While ancient languages account for a vast array of relational connections, the English language has just one word to describe them all: love. As Robert Johnson noted in his classic work *The Fisher King and the Handless Maiden*, using just a single word to express such a wide spectrum of feelings might be limiting the texture and depth of love that we can experience:

> Sanskrit has ninety-six words for love; ancient Persian has eighty, Greek three, and English only one. This is indicative of the poverty of awareness or emphasis that we give to that tremendously important realm of feeling. Eskimos have thirty words for snow, because it is a life-and-death matter to them to have exact information about the element they live with so intimately. If we had a vocabulary of thirty words for love . . . we would immediately be richer and more intelligent in this human element so close to our heart. An Eskimo probably would die of clumsiness if he had only one word for snow; we are close to dying of loneliness because we have only one word for love. Of all

the Western languages, English may be the most lacking when it comes to feeling.

There was probably a time in your life when your experience of loving and being loved was entirely without conditions. You've likely expressed your love to someone or something freely, fully, and without reservation. You've been completely and unrestrictedly attentive, and you have received love in like kind. Perhaps it was when you were an infant; though you might not consciously remember it, you've experienced a quality of love that didn't require you to be someone or something else in order to be lovable.

Children, with their pure hearts and unconditioned minds, are naturally more open to the experience of love. They can look deeply, without defensiveness, into your eyes, whether you are a stranger or a friend to them. Without barriers, defensiveness, and self-doubt, their gaze seems to say, "I'm right here, are you right there?" And love's response is always yes.

True love is that expanded true union, but it requires you to remove all the barriers you have erected to realize it. The barriers are invisible and internal. Love doesn't come from someone or something else; instead, it awakens inside you. And when it does, you realize that you *are* love; you are that which lights the stars.

My Own Early Experiences of Love

When I was a little girl I decided that I was in love with Ricky R., a fellow first grader. This romance was short-lived but exciting. Each afternoon on the bus ride home from school, we'd meet in the back, sit together on the vinyl seat, and kiss each other. I don't know how either of us even learned to kiss, or how first graders would think to do so as a pleasurable activity. But in those moments, when we had each other's attention, I felt excited.

By third grade, I had set my eight-year-old sights on Patrick, a twinkly eyed, brown-haired kid. I don't think he ever looked at me, but I was mesmerized by him. I was convinced that if I could get Patrick to pay attention to me, all would be okay in my world—but Patrick never did. My third-grade self had already started to create beliefs about love: it was completely dependent on another person, and it could be impossible to get.

As I got a little older, TV shows like *Gilligan's Island* and *Bewitched* led me to believe that love in a life like mine wasn't attainable. I'd either have to be stranded on a desert island or attain some special powers in order to find it.

Like a lot of us who were raised in the '60s and '70s, my family didn't talk much about love or romance, or feelings in general for that matter. I never heard the words "I love you" directed toward me or to anyone I knew. Love was a mystery that I was becoming more and more desperate to solve.

Then one autumn, my cousins came to visit and brought me a bright orange kitten as a birthday present. Oh, how I loved her! I felt close and connected to Marmalade. We spent a lot of time together. She'd even run to meet me at the end of the driveway when I got off the bus. But when I was 13, we moved to a new neighborhood across town, and my mother gave Marmalade away.

Right around this same time, my face froze—well, half of it did, anyway. My mother was driving my brother and me to a shopping center, and I realized I couldn't move my face. Thinking that I was being dramatic, she ignored my concern and drove us to a restaurant to get some lunch. As I began to eat, food fell out of my mouth, and I couldn't even drink out of a cup. It was determined that I had Bell's palsy. The doctor explained that my face had probably become paralyzed from stress, and no one could be sure if and when it would go away.

Of course, as a young teen, I so wanted to be accepted in my new neighborhood. I wanted to look normal, make new friends, and even possibly win the boys' attention. But I went unnoticed. Instead, they flocked around the cool girls who sat on the radiator in the lunchroom—the ones who had figured out how to blow-dry their hair into a flip like Farrah Fawcett's. (I hadn't; my hair was impossible.) I felt far from popular or accepted with my frozen face.

A few months later, my face finally started to regain movement. By then my parents had moved from regularly fighting to separating, then finally to divorce. I became more interested in numbing out than in being popular. I spent a lot of time in the art room and the smoking lounge. (Can you believe we had those in high school?) I dressed boyishly in men's vests I'd found in secondhand stores and made few friends—outcasts like myself.

Then, late in my junior year, I discovered the Rivers Country Day School, a private boys' school on the outskirts of town. Though I was never a "Ginger" or "Marianne," when I was there I did feel like one of a small handful of girls shipwrecked on an island populated only by boys. Every time I sneaked onto campus, I became instantly popular. My desire for attention was temporarily satisfied. I dated one boy after another and got the affection I craved.

I believed that everything I needed to feel good about myself and my place in life—namely, attention, affection, approval, and popularity—had to be acquired from outside sources. So, I worked hard to get it, as my emotional well-being depended on it. I felt desperate between relationships and had no idea that I could generate these feelings from within. I held the belief that there wasn't enough love for me and, for some reason, I didn't deserve it anyway. Things got a lot worse before they got better

By the time I was 18, I had joined the Army. On Christmas leave, I found myself standing in front of a justice of the peace, eloping with my then-boyfriend Whitey. The Carpenters' song "We've Only Just Begun" was playing softly from the cassette deck. Although he was a bit older than I was and had been in jail a number of times, he wanted to marry me. Desperate for love and attention, I said yes.

Whitey gave me plenty of attention—but, unfortunately, it was not the kind that made me feel good. It was accompanied by hatred, jealousy, and anger. I soon became the target of my new husband's violence. I had made a terrible mistake, but I couldn't tell anyone; no one knew we were even married.

I stayed with Whitey and reinforced my belief that love and pain went hand in hand. I shut down emotionally and went through my days feeling so very alone. He threatened to kill me if I left him, but after two years, I realized I had no other choice but to take that chance. I gathered my courage, transferred to the National Guard, got my GED, and headed off to college.

Unlike most of the freshmen in my dorm who were just beginning to experience life, I had already been through military service, marriage, and abuse. I couldn't really relate to my class-mates. I was a 21-year-old with poor self-esteem, ashamed of my past and deeply distrustful of my ability to make better choices in the future.

Surrender

In my 30s, I was again brokenhearted after my latest boyfriend lost interest in me. I decided to leave Mount Shasta, where I'd lived and worked for a little over a year after leaving the Zen center. With my Volvo loaded with all my belongings in the trunk, and my two big black dogs sitting in the back seat, I navigated the snow-covered passes with studded snow tires, and headed south to Los Angeles.

L.A. had been a city that was near the top of my "I'll never live there" list. But when the opportunity arose to work with Byron Katie, a woman I considered a great teacher, I took it. I soon became the director of her School for The Work.

When we arrived in Manhattan Beach, I unpacked my things but wasn't able to really settle in because I was house-sitting. I had to board my dogs until I found a home for all of us. It was a tough time; I was heartbroken, my dogs were gone, and I was living in a place I didn't really like (yet).

I meditated every day. But I was still living with a deep-seated belief I hadn't been able to shake: I wasn't lovable. Though I knew that my very nature is love, and I knew life loved me in ways I couldn't even fathom, this deep-seated belief that I was unlovable reared its ugly head anytime I was in or out of an intimate rela-tionship. It followed me everywhere.

I couldn't meditate my heartbreak away. I couldn't transcend it like I usually did. I had to face it. Even though I was lonely, it was obvious that a new relationship wasn't going to be the answer. Neither was going on another journey to an exotic destination to distract myself from my growing disappointment.

This was it. I had finally grown tired of the chain of unfulfilling relationships that were aggravating my instability both inside and out. I was no longer willing to wait to find the perfect relationship or my "soul mate" to enjoy my life and feel good about myself. It was too difficult to be constantly distracted and trying to manipulate external circumstances to find a source of love from outside myself.

I had to stay right where I was and dig in, praying that in doing so I would discover a way that I could feel the love that was already here, inside me. Even if I never found my true love and ended up being single for the rest of my life, I was sure I'd be all right.

For the first time in my life, I focused my attention on being happy while single—a big deal for a serial dater like myself. Gone were my fantasies of falling in love with a perfect someone in order to live happily ever after. Instead, I had a new plan. It was time to change my thinking, make different choices, and challenge the low opinion and criticisms I held about myself that were causing me so much suffering. I was determined to experience the feeling of being "in love" by learning to love myself.

Luckily I was in the right place, working with someone who taught people how to question the thoughts and beliefs that caused suffering—thoughts like *I am unlovable*. Katie would sit with individuals onstage at a workshop or retreat, give them her undivided attention, and ask them to share their thoughts. She'd then have them do The Work, asking four questions to cut through their delusions. I'd watch as these questions changed people's reality.

My belief that I was unlovable was met with the questions: "Is it true? Can you absolutely know it's true?" Well, yes, of course I believed it to be true—but did I know it absolutely? Maybe not.

The next question was, "How do you react when you think this thought?" This question illuminated my past behavior. I didn't make good choices. I behaved badly. I looked for love everywhere and compromised myself to get it. I didn't believe there was enough love for me. *There*: those were the barriers I had built against love.

The last question of the inquiry was, "Who would you be without the thought?" Without the thought *I am unlovable*, I realized I actually felt lovable. I felt open and loving toward others and myself. I felt free from the trap I had set for myself—the trap of depending on others to make me feel loved.

Thoughts are that powerful. A simple thought can hold you hostage or mentally hold someone else hostage. A simple thought can change your life. I had lived with the unquestioned belief that there was something wrong with me, that I was unlovable, and I lived a life that proved it. But it was only a thought; freedom was on the other side of questioning its validity.

Katie spoke with one woman who was doing The Work on her thought that her husband did not love her. "Oh, honey!" she exclaimed. "How can you expect him to know how to love you when you don't know how to love yourself? You have to teach him." This comment enlightened me to my own dilemma. *How could I expect someone to love me when I didn't know how to love myself?*

At that point, I committed to discovering what it truly took to love myself. I even decided to marry myself.

The Perfect Partner

By this point in my life, I had already made many pledges and vows, including those I took in the Army, those I took when I eloped, and those I took as a Zen Buddhist. At the Zen center, I had vowed to save all sentient beings. Now I was vowing to save myself, to love and honor myself, not to leave myself, and to be kind to myself.

How do I hope to be treated by someone who loves me? I asked myself. I came up with a list of ways, and then proceeded to give all of that to myself. I practiced being my own perfect partner.

One item on my list was to buy myself a ring so I didn't have to wait for *the* ring that many women wait for in order to feel worthy. I soon bought myself a pretty sterling silver ring, which was set with a variety of blue stones. Every time I looked at it, it was a reminder to be sweet to myself and to love myself.

Also on my list were the places and activities that I had been waiting for someone to invite me to. So I took myself out on dates to concerts, dinners, walks along the beach, movies, and coffee.

I sang along with the love songs that played on the radio, but I sang them to myself. I stopped saying nasty things to myself each time I walked by a mirror. I stopped berating myself for the choices I had made in the past, and I stopped ceaselessly and ruthlessly comparing myself to others. I continued to remain faithful to my meditation practice, which increased my awareness of the contrasting ways I treated myself. I aimed to be kind and loving versus being self-critical and contracted.

The first tender roots of genuine self-love gradually began to sprout. I stopped holding back what I wanted to say, and practiced getting to know myself and what was really going on within me. I began to say what I really felt instead of what I thought would please others and win me their love and approval. Moment by moment, day by day, I practiced staying true to myself. It was so simple, but I can't say it was easy.

Gradually, I began to feel compassion for all I had put myself through. I felt a genuine concern for myself that I'd never experienced before. My heart began to heal as I opened up to the love that was present with my newly expanded way of walking in the world.

I saw and felt the love everywhere. It radiated from people and nature whether I was at the dog park or the beach, shopping in the grocery store, or visiting the coffee shop. It was in me, too. I was no longer seeing life through a narrow perspective of self-deception and limiting beliefs. As the English poet and philosopher William

Blake wrote, "If the doors of perception were cleansed every thing would appear to man as it is, infinite. For man has closed himself up, till he sees all things thro' narrow chinks of his cavern."

It is difficult to put into words just how much of a revelation this experience was for me. The source of love had been in me all along. Before, I'd known it intellectually; now it was a reality. Love is infinite. Love is the ocean, the sky, the stranger; love is everywhere, beaming through everyone and everything. I found freedom, independence, joy, and peace. I felt a lightness of being that I had only previously tasted in meditation. By my 40th year of life, I felt love inside and out.

The irony of it all is that nothing had changed. Love was there all along. What shifted was my awareness—my intentional attention—that I trained myself to direct toward it. I'd been looking outside of myself for so long that my mind had to be purposefully focused on recognizing the love that surrounds, and is, me.

Marty

Months after making the commitment to marry myself, I met the man I would eventually marry. I was at Katie's home dropping off some papers when she introduced me to Marty, an out-of-town friend of hers who was staying with her. Our conversation was easy. We had a lot in common. It turned out we had lived within miles of each other for years, in neighboring towns outside of Boston. We'd both spent the majority of our adult lives focused on our spiritual paths and our practice of meditation. Each of us was fully committed to where that practice would take us. Though we had different paths and different teachers, we realized right away that we were kindred spirits.

Later, Marty told me that on the same day we'd met, he'd seen me while gazing out the second-story window of Katie's house. I'd been walking down to the beach on one of my solo dates. Marty said that he noticed a blond girl on the sidewalk who was radiant, self-confident, and contented, and *that* was what had attracted him. By the time I met him, it was true, I had grown to love who I was. I felt solid, stable, contented, and present and none of it had anything to do with being loved by someone else. *It just was.*

We got to know each other over the next few months. I started to notice that I felt good about myself and him, both while I was with him and when I wasn't with him.

Though I had been married briefly, I had never been engaged, and I soon realized that it was more important to me than being married. As the word *engaged* suggests, it's an ongoing commitment that should continue long after a wedding ceremony. It's a commitment we would soon make to be present and loving toward ourselves and each other.

Months later, in the fall, I moved to Sedona with my dogs, and a year and a half later, we got married. We made a vow to stay engaged, and to support each other along this winding road toward (what we hope is) enlightenment. Fifteen years have since passed, and we each are still devoted to connecting with the field of love in meditation and being cognizant of this field as it moves through us each and every moment of every day.

Marty's spiritual path is characterized by a heartfelt surrender to the divine feminine energy that he connects with in meditation. He leads silent meditations twice a day almost every day at my meditation center in Sedona.

My spiritual path is based on service. I am committed to creating more peace on Earth through my work, my practice, and my life. I believe that peace on Earth can only be achieved one person, one heart, and one nervous system at a time. I cultivate inner peace with daily meditation, regular self-examination, and the guidance I receive from ancient and modern spiritual teachers and wisdom traditions. I also teach meditation to those who want more peace, and I train teachers of meditation to do the same. These teachers are a cadre for peace.

The Inquiry

Have you ever thought about love, not as a romantic ideal or a prize that is awarded to those who prove themselves worthy, but as a universal force that underlies and sustains all? Whether you have had the most difficult of journeys or are in a wonderful relationship with everyone and everything, you might want to examine your relationship to love itself.

This exercise is an inquiry into your limiting beliefs about love and how those can impede your ability to be present and to realize your true nature. This inquiry requires your courage, honesty, presence, and—above all—kindness toward yourself.

Perhaps, like me, initially you understood love to be something that is gained through the attention of another. Perhaps you think there is not enough love to go around. Perhaps you are the one who gives love and no one seems to notice. Once you identify the misconceptions you have about love and the barriers you have erected between yourself and love, you can then set about removing them. Remember, your intentional attention is truly powerful!

1. First, make a list of your limiting beliefs about love. Use simple, short statements like, "Love hurts," or, "There's not enough love to go around," or, "I will never find someone who will love me."

2. Next, direct the following questions to each of those statements, *one belief* at a time:

- *How do I react when I think this thought? How do I behave? How do I treat myself? How do I treat others when I believe this thought? Where do I feel it in my body?*

- *What do I get for having the thought? What are the payoffs? Do I get to be right? Do I get to feel separate? Do I get to be a victim? Do I get to be better than others?*

- Close your eyes and ask: *Who would I be without the thought?* Spend a few moments basking in the spaciousness of who you would be without the limitations of that belief. It can be similar to the silence experienced when you transcend in meditation.

Be sure to use this inquiry with each and every limiting belief you hold about love. It will reveal and help remove your barriers to love. When you are paying attention, love wakes you up to a reality that is more profound and more perfect than any you have experienced or thought about. Everything, every experience you've ever had, just might suddenly make sense.

3. Lastly, create a list of ways you hope to be treated by someone who loves you, whether a friend, parent, co-worker, partner, or child. Take your time and be thorough. As you review this list, recognize it as your prescription for how to treat yourself so you can know yourself as a loving, worthy being.

With a commitment to sincerely examine what prevents you from knowing love and knowing yourself as love, with a commitment to treating yourself with kindness rather than criticism, and with a commitment to tearing down the barriers of your false beliefs, you'll discover that *you* are the one you have been waiting for. In other words, all along, what you have been looking for is what has been looking.

Chapter 5

The Gift of Contentment

The Sun never says to the Earth, "You owe me." Look what happens with a love like that. It lights up the whole sky.

—HAFIZ

When you are present, open, expanded, and mindful, you are tapped into the unbounded, unlimited supply of love. Rather than seeing love as a finite resource that you have to vie for, hoard, or steal in order to get your share, you *know* it is everywhere and plentiful. Even if you can't sense it outside of yourself, you can always connect with it as you turn your attention inward.

Recently, I was speaking at an event at the Chopra Center in Carlsbad, California, along with Lynne Twist, author of *The Soul of Money*. She talked about the myth of scarcity. "Scarcity is a lie," she stated. "It is independent of any actual amount of resource. It is an unexamined and false system of assumptions, opinions, and beliefs. Scarcity is a perspective by which many of us view the world. We live in a place where we are in constant danger of not having our needs met."

She went on to talk about how many of us, from the moment we open our eyes in the morning, begin our versions of *I don't have enough.*

Perhaps you look at the clock and think, *I didn't sleep enough.* Or maybe you catch your reflection in the mirror and lament, *I don't look good enough/thin enough/rested enough/young enough.* Or when you are in your closet deciding what to wear, you quickly make the determination, *I don't have enough black pants.* And then there's the ever-present, *I don't have enough time.*

Scarcity Rules

The myth of scarcity can easily become a mental habit—the lens through which you view the world. It eventually becomes so familiar that you may never stop to question its validity. I bet you can quickly fill in the blank here: *I don't have enough* _____. (This is also a great belief on which to practice the inquiry exercise from the previous chapter!)

Consider your internal response to hearing the news that someone has had something wonderful happen for them, whether he or she landed the perfect job, received an award, found true love, or experienced some other measure of success that you wish you had. How do you initially respond?

Perhaps you are happy for them. You realize that their success shows that it's possible for each of us to succeed, and there is enough for everyone. But for some who hear about how others experience an abundance of love, money, happiness, recognition, or success, they experience envy, and an arousal of the unconscious belief: *there's not enough for me.*

If you've experienced this, you might be a little ashamed to admit it. But it certainly can and does happen. You become a little envious and feel a slight contraction in your heart. I know that it happens in me when I am not taking great care of myself. It doesn't feel kind or generous to begrudge another's success. After all, I would certainly want someone to be happy for me. And I imagine you'd want someone to be happy for you, too. If you aren't able to be happy for another's success, you can take a look at what is going on in there. *Why am I not able to be generous?*

Some of us believe there's a scarcity of happiness, success, love, or creativity and there is not enough to go around. This scarcity mind-set can rob you of the ability to see all of life as interconnected and to appreciate all that has already been given to you: your body, health, family, friends, shelter, safety, and nourishment. It also prevents you from celebrating that which you have already accomplished.

This scarcity mind-set creates separation and contracts your awareness. There's *I, me,* and *mine,* and then there's *they, them,* and *theirs.* Einstein was once quoted as calling this separation an "optical delusion of consciousness," saying that this delusion of separation serves as a prison, restricting our interests and concerns to our own personal desires and those of people close to us.

The envy and jealousy that this belief in scarcity breeds is depicted in Buddhism with the iconic images of hungry ghosts: horribly ugly creatures with hugely bloated, empty stomachs and necks too thin to allow food to pass. Hungry ghosts seek personal power and will steal and manipulate to get it. They can never, ever be satisfied.

There are those who are trying to fill themselves by amassing wealth, recognition, or attention, or by achieving some sort of status, whether it's through their clothing, their cars, buying more than they need, accumulating more money, or chasing fame. This can be a full-time focus, and not only is it exhausting, it is also an unstable and unsustainable way to live.

Those dependent on externals can become so desperate and uncomfortable that they steal to get what they think they need. It's like going after a drug. On this subject, a few people from Wall Street and Hollywood come to mind. They, in the past, had been celebrated for some culturally agreed-upon successes: fame, wealth, and status. But their success came at an expense. They compromised their values by saying things they didn't believe or acting in ways that only supported their dependency on praise from the outside world. Maybe they believed the end justified the means. It's not called "selling your soul" for nothing. I imagine it is a horrible way to live. These people were and continue to be exposed. Some of them are now in jail. That's because the hungry ghost is greedy.

Not everyone who is needy is greedy. But when you are insecure and strive to gain attention and/or approval from someone "out there," you can be left feeling unsatisfied, even if you do get what you want. It's as if you "leave" yourself in order to garner others' approval or appreciation. And this creates more of a need because you're empty inside.

When you don't leave yourself, you'll find the source of your own happiness, security, love, peace, attention, and appreciation is already inside you. It's *what* is looking through your eyes. As Julie, the manager of our meditation teacher-training program, says, "Don't outsource your happiness."

Some people seek careers that they are not passionate about because they offer some sort of status. Others marry someone they don't truly love in pursuit of material security or the approval of others. Others say what they don't mean because they want to be accepted. Whenever you override what matters to you in favor of others' opinions or wishes, you can gradually become alienated from the subtle nuances of your interior world. You lose yourself, becoming less committed to your values, less aware of what you really need, less able to speak your truth, and less able to tap into your own centerpoint of peace. You become distracted from your real life. This is when dis-integration occurs. It is the opposite of integrity, and it creates suffering.

I believe that each one of us has a benevolent nature, even if we've consciously or unconsciously erected barriers between our personality and the truth of who we are. Fortunately, these barriers can be dismantled. You can uncover the truth of who you are and reconnect with your true essence—that aspect of you that *is* enough, is already successful, and is already satisfied. That is your very nature; in truth, you don't need to gain anything from "out there."

Byron Katie offers this prayer for those of us who are suffering due to not being able to source our own contentment: "God spare me from the desire to seek love, approval, and appreciation." And I would add to that: "attention."

The Yogic Perspective

The philosophy of yoga also offers lessons for us on love and contentment. It's important to know that yoga is so much more than the common Western notion of twisting into physical postures on a mat. It is a specific science of expanding and uniting your awareness with every part of yourself: your body, your mind, and your extended body—the environment. The word *yoga* comes from the Sanskrit *yuj*, meaning "to yoke, join, or unite." Yoga is a way of life that leads to the ultimate integration: uniting your individual awareness with that of the eternal, universal One. This union creates self-realization, freedom, and an awakening to love.

The roots of yoga can be traced back to Vedic times, roughly 5,000 years ago, in the Indus River Valley civilization. Its philosophy and practices were passed on as an oral tradition through an unbroken line of gurus and disciples who recited *sutras* in Sanskrit. A sutra is a short phrase, a seed of wisdom through which the sages taught. This tradition preserved the teachings throughout the centuries until Patanjali, the father of modern yoga, eventually wrote them down.

Patanjali lived sometime between 200 B.C.E. and 200 C.E. He compiled 195 sutras that laid out the philosophy and practices of yoga. *The Yoga Sutras of Patanjali* is the original yoga guidebook that many (including I) refer to today. In it, he describes the eight limbs of yoga—eight areas of focus that include guidelines for social conduct and self-regulating behaviors, personal practices, physical postures, breathing exercises, withdrawal of the senses, mindfulness, meditation, and, the goal of yoga, *samadhi*—union with the field of love.

One of the yogic principals of social conduct is *asteya*, which means "non-stealing." Asteya describes a way of living in which you don't take anything that's not freely given. It's living with the knowing that you have enough, and feeling supported and satisfied with what is.

When you believe that you don't have enough, feel as though you're not enough, or think that there isn't enough for you, you might aim to fill the emptiness by taking what does not belong to you. I'm not just talking about material objects that haven't been freely offered; I am also talking about nontangible things such as love, attention, opportunity, trust, peace, or energy from others. Can you think of ways in which someone has taken these from you, or you have taken them from others? It could have happened in your relationships at home or at work when you felt deceived or misled or taken advantage of.

These mental habits, especially those consistent with not having enough or needing more, will steal your own attention from your real life. They distract you from the present moment—where you actually are and what you already enjoy—and propel your focus into the future as you muse about how you are going to get whatever it is you think will fill you up.

Attention Is the Antidote

One way to establish the conduct of asteya and reduce cravings and endless desirousness is to become more attentive to your life right here, right now. You can cultivate attentiveness with mindfulness practices and meditation. As you learned in Chapter 2, being mindful is a practice of deliberately being present to what you are doing, feeling, and thinking, without judgment. It's a way of living as a human *being* rather than a human *doing*.

By being present, you can appreciate what you already have, who is in front of you, and the life you are living. You realize that happiness isn't dependent on some future goal being met. This doesn't mean you don't have goals or plans, but it does mean you won't be obsessed with them or wait to be engaged or attentive to your life. In other words, they won't take up your entire attentional bandwidth.

When you are paying attention, you are alert to sensations of physical or emotional comfort and discomfort. An emotion, pleasant or unpleasant, arises in response to a thought. It's important to pay attention to your emotions, notice them, and allow them to come and go. Let them have their life. Feel them. Bear witness to them. Don't make your emotions anyone else's problem or responsibility. Your emotions are yours to feel. If uncomfortable emotions recur, they are the key to letting you know that you believe a thought that probably isn't true, such as, *I am not enough*, *They are more deserving than I am*, or *There is not enough for me*.

Each emotion generates a sensation in your body. Sensation is the way your body, aka your best friend, communicates with you. So it's important to listen to what it wants to say. Welcome each sensation as it arises, without a story or judgment. Meet it with curiosity, compassion, and inquiry. You can ask yourself, *Where do I feel it? What does the sensation feel like? What is this feeling communicating to me? Where does this feeling arise from?*

Your body doesn't lie. It will let you know if you are relaxed, calm, confident, stressed, or harried. When you really pay attention, your body will let you know when you've said something you don't mean, someone else is telling you a lie, or your attention is being hijacked by some self-limiting belief. It will also let you know when you are envious of someone else's success, if you believe you don't have enough, or if you are taking something that doesn't belong to you.

When you pay attention to your emotions and your body's responses, it is like hooking up to a trusty biofeedback machine. With awareness, you can undo the mythology of scarcity.

Choice Is the Antidote: Two Wolves

Some of us walk around with a myriad of self-defeating thoughts—you know, the thoughts that make you lose faith in yourself and in others. They play in a loop, and with each repetition they are affirmed, creating a well-worn neuronal highway in your brain. But you can change all that by changing what you pay attention to; take your attention off of negative thoughts and replace them with thoughts that support your happiness.

For instance, you can replace a negative thought with a positive affirmation such as: *I am enough, I appreciate my life, I have enough*, or *I am content.* To get the most out of an affirmation, the key is to use short, positive statements in the present tense (not the future). By repeating affirmations, you not only create a new mental habit, but also reframe your entire perspective. Some affirmations can remind you (re-*mind*—get it?) that you are enough and there is enough for everyone. There is more than enough attention, opportunity, trust, and love in this world for everyone—and that includes you. All you have to do is pay attention and affirm it.

There's a Native American legend that illustrates the power of attention: An old man is teaching his grandson about life. "A fight is going on inside me," he says to the boy. "It's a terrible fight between two wolves. One is evil—he is anger, envy, sorrow, regret, greed, arrogance, self-pity, guilt, resentment, inferiority, lies, false pride, superiority, and ego. The other is good—he is joy, peace, love, hope, serenity, humility, kindness, benevolence, empathy, appreciation, generosity, truth, compassion, and faith. The same fight is going on inside you—and inside every other person, too."

The child thinks about it and asks, "Which wolf will win?"

His grandfather replies, "The one you feed."

You will soon be so attuned to your mental habits that when you notice that you are focusing on or feeding something that doesn't feel good, you'll have the real-time ability to reclaim your attention and shift your focus toward something more supportive. What you look for, you will find. If you are looking for the bounty and wonder of life, you'll find it, because your attention will make it come alive to you.

Appreciation Is the Antidote

Another antidote to the scarcity mind-set is to focus your attention on what you already have. Remember, what you put your attention on grows! Look around and appreciate everything that supports you right in this moment. Is there enough? When you look for it, there certainly is. From where does all of this support arise?

When I'm leading meditation retreats, I often ask students to contemplate how much time, energy, and resources went into the making of the clothes they are wearing, the chair they are sitting on, and the food they enjoyed at their last meal. The students begin to realize the many ways they are being cared for and loved, and how many people, most of them perfect strangers, work on their behalf each and every day.

Appreciation turns what you think you don't have enough of into plenty. When you live with your attention focused on the abundance around you, it will transform your notion of scarcity into gratitude. A newfound sense of abundance can be cultivated, because whatever you look for, you will find. Whatever you put your gentle loving attention on grows.

It's true that there are national days dedicated to appreciation, such as Mother's Day, Father's Day, and Thanksgiving. I did a little research and found many other "appreciation days," both official and unofficial, such as employee appreciation day, client appreciation day, and teacher appreciation day. You may have heard of or participated in days of appreciation for police officers, firefighters, volunteers, active-duty military members, and military spouses. (Apparently, appreciation days exist even for cows, barbershop music, beer cans, and houseplants!) However, you don't have to wait for a special day to be appreciative. You can put your attention on and appreciate everything and everyone you set your eyes on *today.*

Appreciate everything you taste, smell, feel, and hear. Appreciate your ability to sense all these things. Appreciate your ability to move, dance, love, and think. Appreciate your freedom and imagination, and your ability to make choices. Appreciate being able to read whatever you like and say whatever you mean. Appreciate your compassion and creativity. Appreciate your family, friends, those in your workplace, and the devices that keep you connected. The list is endless; there is so much to be thankful for.

Appreciation Meditation

Before beginning the following meditation, bring your focus to your heart. It does much more than pump blood through your veins; it is the center of wisdom in your body. There are as many neurons in your heart as there are in some sections of your brain; in fact, the heart's magnetic field is actually 5,000 times stronger.

The heart is wise. Turn your attention to its beating. Now focus your attention on the area behind your breastbone, enlivening your heart center and its qualities of peace, love, compassion, joy, gratitude, and inclusiveness.

This heart-centered appreciation meditation can be done with your eyes open or closed. I suggest you first practice it as an open-eyed meditation exercise. You can do it wherever you are, anytime; simply relax your body wherever you are sitting. You'll need about 10 minutes, though you can do it for as long as you like.

There is no need to force a feeling; instead, be present to what you feel as you read these words and follow the prompts.

Bring your attention to your breath as you breathe naturally through your nose. Feel the sensations of the inhale and exhale: the coolness of your breath on the inhale, the warmth on the exhale.

Scan your body to be sure you are completely relaxed.

Let your attention rest on the rise and fall of your chest. Notice your heart beating or any subtle sensations that are present.

Just behind your breastbone, see, feel, or imagine your heart center. Let your attention rest there for a breath or two.

Imagine your breath moving into and out of your heart center. (You can place your hand over the center of your chest, on your breastbone, to help keep your attention focused there.)

Appreciate your commitment to being more loving, more attentive, and more powerful.

Appreciate your body and how it serves and supports you.

Tune in to the wisdom of your body: your heartbeat, your breath. Consider the effortless intelligence that orchestrates this beautiful symphony of your life.

You are being taken care of in every single moment. You are being taken care of right now.

The whole universe is conspiring to wake you up to the love that you are and to your potential.

Look around the room you're sitting in and notice what surrounds you. See how it all serves you by making your life easier, more enjoyable, and more beautiful.

Appreciate your home and how it offers you safety, security, and comfort.

Your home, the furniture in it, and the clothes on your body—all these gifts are made possible by the efforts of other humans on your behalf. Appreciate their labor and their service to your life.

Allow your attention to expand to the world outside your home and into the natural world. Appreciate the natural resources that surround and support you, which make your life possible. Appreciate the creatures that share this earth with you. Appreciate the elements of fire, light, earth, wind, water, and space.

If it's daytime and light is streaming through your window, appreciate the life-giving power of the sun.

Tune in to the air that you are breathing, the earth underneath you.

Appreciate whatever and whoever else is keeping you company in this moment.

There is so much, right here, right now, to appreciate.

When you are finished, sit silently for a few moments with your eyes closed. Let your attention still rest on your heart center for a few minutes. Take your time before opening your eyes and engaging in activity.

When you pay attention in this way, you start to realize that you already have more than enough. Remember, what you look for, you will find. Look for the ways in which you are supported in this life. Notice and appreciate all you already have, do, and are. What a way to live!

Tuning In to Gratitude

According to research on gratitude, those who practice being grateful experience more vitality and optimism and higher levels of positive emotions. They have a greater capacity for empathy and are viewed by others as more generous and more helpful.

Researcher and psychologist Dr. Robert Emmons of the University of California, Berkeley, says that those who have cultivated gratitude and appreciation for life can "experience an overall shift to a more benevolent view of the world. I think it's kind of a spiritual shift for some people because it makes them more aware of life as a gift."

Research also finds that those who appreciate their lives feel responsible for and committed to the well-being of others. Grateful people place less importance on their own material wealth and are less likely to judge others based on what they have. They are more likely to share what they have with others who don't have as much. In general, they are more satisfied with life.

Making a list or keeping a journal are simple ways to cultivate gratitude. It's easy to do; simply set aside 10 minutes every day to write down what you are grateful for. You can do this when you wake up or right before you go to sleep. I often lie in bed and mentally list 10 things before going to sleep, or I do it right when I wake up. It's easy when you put your attention on it. Simply let your imagination wander to everyone who supports you in this life, to those who work on your behalf, and to this beautiful planet that makes life possible.

Cultivating Contentment

Contentment is another area explored in the Yoga Sutras. The word for it is *santosha*. It's a practice of being content with who you are, what you have, and what's happening around you. It is said that practicing santosha leads to unsurpassable happiness. And who doesn't want to be unsurpassably happy?

Though you might hope to attain something more or accomplish a particular goal, there is no need to wait for a certain set of circumstances to be met in order to feel content. Contentment means being comfortable with and accepting of yourself, of others, and of the circumstances of your life as they are right now.

Santosha creates inner stability because it doesn't depend on anything external, such as an event, an achievement, someone's approval or attention, or possessing the next item. As my friend Kenny Loggins sings, "This is it; make no mistake where you are. The waiting is over." Do not wait for happiness; do not wait to feel content. *You are the one the world is waiting for.* Don't wait to generously offer yourself freely to the world. Do it right now, whether you feel ready or not. Contentment leads to generosity of spirit.

My grandmother Bertha seemed to embody santosha. When I was young, she seemed elfish, standing just a little taller than I at 4 feet 11 inches. Grammie had twinkly eyes, a melodic voice, and long gray hair that she braided and pinned at the top of her head. She made her own clothes, hand-sewing dresses and knitting sweaters. Every evening, she knitted or crocheted something, whether it was a sweater, an afghan, or a scarf, many of which she'd give to her friends or grandchildren.

She collected seashells and pinecones and created gorgeous wreaths with them for every season. They adorned the doors of family and friends, and a huge one hung on the doors of the church where she played a giant pipe organ every Sunday. In decent weather she walked barefoot out to her gardens to attend to her prize-winning begonias and select flowers for her stunning arrangements. She was the president of the New England Garden Club, and her gardens were vibrant and impressive. She pressed and dried the smaller flowers for her Christmas cards. She provided a home for the many kittens abandoned in nearby fields that were fortunate enough to make their way to her back door. I was in awe of her communion with and reverence for the natural world and of the creativity that it inspired in her.

On May Day each year, I'd help her make May baskets for her neighbors, friends, and those who needed cheering up. Each one contained a mini flower arrangement and a few culinary delights from her kitchen. She was popular for her blueberry muffins made with wild blueberries picked in the nearby woods and the blackberry jam she jarred from berries picked off the brambles in the field out back.

When delivering her May baskets, she taught me how to greet everyone, whether they were strangers or friends. She showed me how to reach out and hold someone's hand and ask how they were. She taught me to say "please" and "thank you" and mean it. Her life was an endless offering as she connected with and cared for so many, simply for the joy it brought her. Her contentment and generosity of spirit continues to inspire me in so many ways.

Generosity of Spirit

Being attentive and generous simply because it feels good to give is natural when you're content. When I'm training students to become teachers of meditation, I give them an assignment to perform random acts of kindness for five days. Invariably, the first few acts of kindness seem to benefit someone they know: "I gave my husband a massage." "I put a love note in my child's lunch." "I offered my elderly neighbor a ride." The world is a kinder place when we reach out to help or attend to someone else, no doubt.

Next, I will suggest that they perform an *anonymous* act of kindness. They then have to identify a recipient (a person, a community, an animal, or even some aspect of the natural world) without evaluating whether they are "deserving" of the kindness. The deed has to be done without the recipient knowing who they are, and without telling a single soul (except for me). This task can be tough on the ego, illuminating how attached we can be to receiving appreciation or recognition.

Kindness Calls

The Dalai Lama has been quoted as saying, "If you want others to be happy, practice compassion. If you want to be happy, practice compassion."

Compassion is natural. It's motivated by a desire to relieve the suffering of those who share this planet with us. It is love in action. When you are paying attention, you will be alert to the internal impulses to generously and unconditionally lend a helping hand; you'll be alert to the call to be compassionate. When you give without expecting anything in return—neither appreciation nor recognition—you become more intimate with the field of love as it moves you to serve others. Compassion is not a concept; it's a reality.

You don't even have to think about it. You simply have to be present and open. You'll feel moved, and you can then respond to this call. It's one way that you, like the sun, can radiate your love and your light unconditionally. Being compassionate is expansive and liberating beyond description.

I encourage you to try it for yourself. Here are some simple ideas: Pay for the meal of the person behind you in the drive-through line. Return someone's shopping cart to the cart corral for them. Give flowers to someone you don't know. Visit a local nursing home and bring your favorite poem to share or a deck of cards to play a game with a resident. Put a quarter in an expired parking meter. Write a letter to a teacher who made a difference in your life. Put your phone away while waiting in line and start a conversation with a stranger. Let someone have the parking space you were both eyeing.

Your acts of kindness can also be for the benefit the planet as you consciously create a smaller carbon footprint in consideration of the well-being of the generations of children that will come after you: Host a clean-up party at the beach or park. When you buy single-use paper products such as copy paper, paper cups, toilet paper, and paper towels, make sure that they are made from recycled materials, even if they are a little more expensive. Use less plastic. Recycle everything you can, and reuse what you can. Cut down on buying things you don't need. Donate usable items that you were saving for another day. Start a carpool. Plant a few trees. Grow a garden. Buy organic, locally grown produce to reduce pesticide use and transportation emissions and support local farmers. Pick up trash on your walks. Lobby for an environmental cause. Speak for those who can't. Bring mindfulness into each action and notice how you feel before, during, and after each act of kindness

Compulsion to Give

Seeing another being in a state of hardship, discomfort, or need can cause a strong desire within you to give something—whether it's a caring hand, a supportive word, or a material resource, such as food, money, or a jacket. And of course it's kind. But is it the right move for you?

When your action is motivated by an urge to soothe your own feelings of guilt, shame, or obligation, it is not being freely given—and giving it may not even be kind. Though on the surface it may appear to be a selfless act, it could be that you are expecting something from the transaction—a thank-you, perhaps, or to be seen as generous, or to feel better about yourself. The underlying motivation might be a compulsion to act in order to ease your own discomfort.

An act that looks like generosity on its surface can sometimes be an expression of scarcity; we're "stealing" a feeling of happiness or a sense of relief by offering something to another. It's a subtle distinction to get hold of; perhaps sharing an experience I had recently will illustrate the point:

I had to run to the grocery store to get some fruit for the students' break at a training and I didn't have much time. I was already stressed. It was a chilly winter day, and as I hurried from the parking lot into the store, I passed a homeless man sitting outside on the cold concrete with a dog that I presumed was his. He was skinny, dressed in a lightweight shirt, and his face was covered with scabs. Clearly, he was in bad shape.

Inside the store, I grabbed a bag of food for the dog, a container of soup for him, and a bag of oranges for my class. While paying for the groceries, I asked for his items to be bagged separately. Perhaps I wanted to be seen as a hero or an inspiration, or maybe I wanted to gain some recognition for doing a good deed, as I explained to the employees that there was a man and his dog outside who seemed desperate and homeless.

Although the comment seemed innocent enough, it really wasn't. And probably because the unconscious compulsion to give was in action, I got an unexpected response.

Instead of inspiring the cashier and the woman who was bagging my groceries to feel sympathy, it inspired them to emphatically tell me all the reasons why he didn't deserve the help: *He's just a charlatan. He probably makes more money than we do, anyway. He should go get a job like the rest of us.*

I was flustered and asked if they had even seen the man I was talking about—they hadn't. They'd just assumed, based on the label "homeless," that they already knew everything about him.

Feeling a little off balance, I went outside and handed the man the bag of dog food. He looked at it and let me know that his dog didn't eat *that kind* of dog food, he ate a much better brand. (And, no, I hadn't even bought the cheapest bag!) I was caught off guard and became even more flustered.

"Are you vegetarian?" I asked him reticently. I had bought soup with meat in it, and the way things were going, that was probably a mistake, too. He said he wasn't and took the container of soup without looking at me. My heart was racing as I rushed back to the training.

There was a lesson here, I knew.

When I examined my motivations, I found that I'd wanted to help this guy in order to gain something in return. Although much of this was unconscious, the sensations in my body provided clear feedback that my motivations for wanting to contribute to this man's well-being were not entirely pure.

While there are no hard-and-fast guidelines for assessing your motivation to give, examining what moves you can reveal whether the desire to give is love expressing itself through you spontaneously, or is arising from a compulsion to feel better about yourself. If you really pay attention, selfish motivations don't feel very good.

If your kindness is a reaction to feeling obligated or is rooted in a desire to be seen as a hero or a savior, your urge to give could be a veiled need to receive recognition. On the other hand, if you feel genuinely summoned, inspired to action, and called to respond—in the same way you would instinctively lend a hand to a child—this is a sign that you are being moved by love rather than called by your ego. It can be that subtle.

I had no idea what was going on while it was happening, but since I was so uncomfortable, I had to take a look. I am committed to peace, and I know peace begins with me. And so if I feel compelled to give yet my heart isn't open, I'll truly examine my motive before I cause that kind of ripple effect again.

Cultivating Self-Love

Okay, I'm not perfect, and yet here I am writing this book about the power of attention and awakening to love. But I can tell you I've journeyed far and wide to get where I am today. I do live more mindfully, but alas, I am human. The good news is I have learned to love myself and my humanity no matter what condition I find myself in. Love, by its very nature, is unconditional.

If you haven't yet learned to be compassionate, generous, or patient toward yourself, or if you don't enjoy your own company, you will have a difficult time being compassionate, generous, or patient toward others. This disregard for yourself will also prevent you from actualizing love.

I heard a story about a group of American Tibetan Buddhist teachers who visited the Dalai Lama. They asked him a question about how to work with self-hatred. He didn't understand what they were saying and kept asking his translator to clarify what they meant. Once he understood the concept, he asked the teachers if any of them had personally experienced self-hatred. Many said yes, they had. Not only had they experienced it, it was also the most prevalent obstacle they encountered in the course of teaching their students.

Self-hatred was a concept the Dalai Lama had not been familiar with because it is not typically experienced in Buddhist cultures. Many believe in reincarnation, and being born a human is a good enough reason itself to cherish your life. Now, he frequently says that we can't truly offer compassion to other people until we develop compassion for ourselves. With this in mind, perhaps you'll see the phrase "Love thy neighbor as thyself" in a new light.

Some struggle with self-compassion because they believe it could make them weak or passive or will somehow reduce their motivation to achieve more or reach their goals. I can assure you, it won't. Some believe if they are "too nice" to themselves they'll avoid taking personal responsibility for their choices. Research shows the opposite is true. Others are afraid that if they love themselves, they might become self-indulgent, selfish, or self-absorbed. No one wants to be that way.

Instead, self-compassion is simply compassion turned inward. It's offering yourself unconditional affection and regard. It's loving yourself as you would love a good friend. You give yourself a break and the benefit of the doubt rather than being critical. Self-compassion means loving and embracing every part of you, rather than distancing yourself from your imperfections and mistakes.

For instance, instead of looking for what's wrong, choose to see all that you've done right. Be nicer to yourself. Instead of focusing on how others treat you or feel about you, or trying to please or compare yourself to others, you can take your power back by noticing how you are treating yourself. How do you feel about *you*? How do your feelings about yourself affect the way you treat others? Honor yourself and others by being honest.

Having compassion for yourself is essential. It allows you to be present to your stressful thoughts and painful feelings without repressing them, blaming others for them, or hating yourself for having them. It helps you to navigate the ups and downs of love and loss, of aging and sickness. It strengthens your relationship with your interior realm and, with it, your resilience to weather the impact of the external world.

It's important to note that self-compassion is distinct from self-esteem. Self-esteem is a conditional acceptance of oneself based on achievements, talents, social status, and external measures. It has nothing to do with loving yourself simply because you exist. Self-esteem does not build emotional intelligence, nor does it help us to stay present or centered in the midst of stress or painful feelings.

It's the responsibility of each of us to cultivate self-compassion and self-love so we can self-soothe when we feel lonely, rejected, or misunderstood, and so we can expand our ability to love others as we love ourselves. Love and comfort are already here. They are who we are; we simply have to connect with them.

Loving Kindness Meditation

Loving Kindness Meditation (LKM) is a simple heart-centered meditation technique that anyone of any age can do. The roots of LKM are in Tibetan Buddhism, but it is practiced around the world by people of every faith. This meditation is formally done while sitting down with eyes closed, but it can also be practiced anytime, even when you are in the midst of activity.

This practice helps you see yourself as you really are: capable of giving and receiving love, sweetness, and peace, no matter where you've been, who has hurt you, what you have done to yourself or others, or how you've judged yourself. LKM helps you conquer any sense of separation, fear of intimacy, or fear of love.

Research has shown that the practice of LKM decreases activation in areas of the brain that support negative feelings about ourselves and others, while simultaneously cultivating areas of the brain associated with romantic love, empathy, and compassion. Studies also suggest that LKM can slow the markers of aging; decrease symptoms of PTSD among veterans; and lessen the symptoms of depression, migraine pain, and chronic low-back pain.

You don't need to meditate for long periods of time to experience the benefits, either. Noticeable shifts have been seen after only 10 sessions of 10 minutes each. Those who practice for longer periods are rewarded with even greater results. Practiced regularly, LKM activates your compassionate heart and creates equanimity, generosity, and kindness toward everyone, without regard for how they are related to you, what they believe, or their past actions.

To practice LKM, you'll first need to select a compassionate phrase. You'll use this phrase in meditation, directing it toward others and yourself. (Remember that your attention and the intention that accompanies it have an effect, no matter how far away you may be from those you are focusing on. Your attention is that powerful.) Choose one of the following, if it feels natural, or come up with one in your own words:

- *May you be happy and free from suffering.*

- *May you be free of pain and sorrow.*

- *May you be peaceful and at ease.*

- *May you feel loved.*

- *May you be filled with loving kindness.*

- *May you feel safe and cared for.*

- *May you find true happiness and joy.*

- *May you awaken to your true Self.*

Read through the following instructions. Review them again before your practice. It's natural not to remember each and every step, but as time goes by, the practice will become second nature.

- Before you start, determine how long you'll be doing this practice. Plan for an integration period of a few minutes afterward.

- Keep track of the time with a clock, watch, or meditation timer. Do not set an alarm that you will have to get up to shut off: no kitchen timers, no alarm clocks!

- Find a comfortable position sitting up. Your spine should be upright and your hips should be higher than your knees. Your hands can rest on your lap or knees. You don't have to hold them in any certain position. (Note that although this meditation is formally done while sitting with your eyes closed, as laid out in these instructions, you can also practice it anytime, even when you are engaged in an activity.)

- Do your best to release any expectations of what you "should" experience. Approach the practice with a beginner's mind, allowing whatever happens to happen.

- If your mind wanders, notice what has captured your attention and then gently return to the practice. It doesn't matter how many times this occurs. Remember, it's a practice.

- Do not force a particular feeling or attempt to get rid of unpleasant or undesirable feelings. Instead, bear witness to any emotions that arise. This allows your awareness to expand so you can notice where you withhold your generous heart or have conditions on giving or receiving love and kindness. With this awareness and kindness toward yourself, all conditions can dissipate.

Close your eyes or gaze softly downward. Relax your body. (If during the meditation you need to shift your position, please feel free to do so mindfully.)

Begin by breathing deeply. Inhale slowly and deeply through your nostrils, and visualize your body expanding in 360 degrees. Exhale slowly and fully through your nostrils.

Do this three times, then return to your breath's natural rhythm and depth.

Scan each area of your body, releasing any tension as you go, from the top of your head down to the bottoms of your feet.

Avoid telling yourself a story about any sensations that arise. Simply feel the sensations themselves, then continue.

Bring your attention to your breathing once again. Notice the cool air as you inhale, and the warmer breath as you exhale. Notice the pauses between the breaths. Don't try to control or regulate it. Let it be natural.

Bring your attention to the rise and fall of your chest. Notice your heartbeat and the sensations of being alive.

Bring to your heart/mind someone you care about or who has deeply cared for you, such as a child, parent, partner, or any other being you feel love for. Get a feel for their presence as you visualize them or silently say their name. Feel the warm feelings that you have toward them, then silently and sincerely offer them loving kindness using the phrase you chose.

Allow yourself to sink into and feel whatever emotions arise: love, sadness, bliss, gratitude, and so on. There's no need to force a feeling or make anything up. Be aware and present to whatever experience is happening, even if it feels like nothing at all. Continue in this way for a few minutes.

Refocus your attention on your heart. Now, with the same sincerity, offer the same phrase of compassion to yourself. Practice this for a few minutes. If sensations arise, simply acknowledge their presence. Don't ignore them, cover them up, or attempt to change them. Bear witness to the actual experience for the next few minutes.

Now identify a neutral person—someone you may have met briefly, such as a bus driver, a supermarket cashier, or a delivery person. Even without knowing their name, get a sense of them, imagining their face and what they were doing when you encountered them. Offer this person the same phrase of compassion. Imagine their receiving this blessing and it lightening their load.

Bear witness to what you feel for the next few minutes. Sometimes emotions such as anger, grief, or sadness may arise—a sign that your heart is opening and revealing what is there. (If this gets too difficult, you can shift to one of the mindfulness practices you learned. However, I encourage you to continue with this practice, welcoming all that you feel.)

Now, scan your body to be sure you are still comfortable and relaxed. Bring your attention to your heart center for a few breaths.

Identify someone with whom you've had difficulty over the past few days. Get a feeling for their presence, then offer them the same phrase of compassion. Know that even if they hurt you in the past, you can't fully know what they face in their own life. Imagine that they are receiving this blessing and it lightens their load. Take your time. This may be challenging for you, but remember, it is a practice. Notice what you are feeling, whether it's pleasant, unpleasant, or nothing at all.

After a few minutes, relax and return your focus to your heart center.

Now identify someone or something you believe is suffering or in need. This can be a neighbor, an acquaintance, or even a stranger. You might choose someone whose suffering you've only read or heard about, perhaps in a news story about a natural or man-made disaster. (You can even practice compassion as you direct it toward other forms of life, such as a pet, a wild animal, or an ecosystem.) Offer them the same phrase of compassion.

Don't get hung up in the story of someone's or something's suffering. Instead, consider that they have some of the same daily concerns that you do. Simply keep your attention on them. Imagine their benefiting from your attention. Stay with it for a few minutes.

Expand your awareness to include all beings in your immediate environment. Continue expanding your awareness to include the people in your home, then your neighborhood, then your city. Extend your practice to include all beings on Earth.

When the time is up, keep your eyes closed. Continue to sit in the stillness for a few minutes. Take your time coming out of the meditation, breathing deeply, and stretching into the space around you. Open your eyes slowly, first with a downward gaze, and then opening them all the way.

Widening the Circle

I believe that each one of us can and will awaken to the fact that we are each an individual expression of the field of love and an expression of "the soul of the whole . . . to which every part and particle is equally related: the eternal One," as Emerson said. And though we might seem separate because of our limited sensory perception, we are strung together like beads on a string of love.

In fact, trying to separate us is like trying to view "geysers in a fountain as separate from the water out of which they flow." This is how Michael Talbot illustrated the theory of 20th-century physicist David Bohm. Bohm's theory was that the universe is a hologram. This means that, as with anything constructed holographically, when you take it apart or break it into pieces, you don't get pieces of what it is made up of; instead, you get smaller versions of the whole.

Einstein, one of Bohm's predecessors, had the same perspective. He insisted that seeing everything as separate is a delusion and that, "Our task must be to free ourselves from this prison by widening our circle of compassion to embrace all living creatures and the whole of nature in its beauty." He also conceded that, "Nobody is able to achieve this completely, but the striving for such achievement is in itself a part of the liberation and a foundation for inner security."

When you source compassion, love, and kindness for yourself from within, you will be freed from your co-dependence on external measures. The world becomes a much friendlier place, and you have fewer conditions about what you need to be happy. As you appreciate all that supports you and recognize your own innate benevolence, you'll find that you are easily content. Your contentment is the wellspring of your generosity of spirit and you become more loving, not only toward yourself, but also toward every other living thing on this planet.

A genuine concern and compassion for all beings awakens in you. You feel connected to everyone and everything, everywhere: all species and all kingdoms. The experience of *who you are* shifts from someone who is *seeking* love—from people, from experiences, from material objects—to the realization that *you are* love. You are a living, breathing expression of a field of love, the source from which all of creation arises and returns.

The goal of the Yoga Sutras, samadhi, is to unite your individual awareness with that of the eternal, universal One. You too can create that lasting awareness of the fusion between you and the object of your loving attention—no matter who or what that might be, including yourself. The separation diminishes through your attention, intention, and willingness to free yourself from the prison of self-imposed illusion.

Chapter 6

Darkest Before the Dawn

In the happy night, In secret, when none saw me,
Nor I beheld aught, Without light or guide,
save that which burned in my heart.
This light guided me More surely than the light of noonday
To the place where he (well I knew who!) was awaiting me—
A place where none appeared.
Oh, night that guided me, Oh, night more lovely than the dawn,
Oh, night that joined Beloved with lover,
Lover transformed in the Beloved!

—JOHN OF THE CROSS

Every time you've experienced a significant breakdown, every time you've felt your heart break—whether it was the result of a traumatic event such as the loss of a loved one, a physical challenge, a separation or divorce, or difficulties at work, or an inner experience of loneliness, depression, unworthiness, or disconnection—and you lost contact with the benevolence of the universe, in all actuality, what was happening was that love was aiming to recapture your attention so you could wake up to it.

Whether you fully realize it yet or not, life loves you. It loves you so much, in fact, that it will chase you down, as many times and by whatever means necessary, to awaken you to the field of love. It is conspiring and orchestrating events and circumstances to shake you up and break your heart wide open in order to enlighten you to your true nature: unbounded, unconditioned love.

If you live your life without paying solid attention to what really matters to you, or are entering relationships or experiences without being mindful, and yet you pray to have a better life and to know yourself more, you will likely experience a wake-up call. Sometimes, this wake-up call is what mystics call a "dark night of the soul." It is a point in your journey when love gets your attention, one way or another, and life brings you to your knees—figuratively, and sometimes quite literally.

Jewel in the Lotus

Perhaps you have experienced a time when the old way of living no longer works—and though you've glimpsed a new way, it hasn't yet been revealed completely. During this time of confusion, you can lose your faith and question whether or not there is a place for you in this world. You can feel lonely and overwhelmed. It's as if you've been completely defeated, or forgotten by God (however you define "God").

I wonder if the Dalai Lama has ever felt deserted. I wonder if his teachers forewarned him of the immense challenges, grief, and heartbreak he would face on his spiritual journey—the death threats, the genocide of 1.2 million fellow Tibetans, and the loss of his homeland. His home is no longer Tibet, and it's been that way for half a century. It's now in McLeod Ganj, a beautiful mountainside village in Northern India that once served as a British hill station. This area is a Tibetan cultural center and an area of refuge for Tibetan Buddhists who also escaped persecution in China. In 1960, Jawaharlal Nehru, who was the prime minister of India at the time, offered it to them as a safe haven. It's a peaceful place where Tibetan Buddhists can freely practice their religion and culture in safety.

The day I arrived in McLeod Ganj, I noticed a dramatic difference between this part of India and the south, where I'd traveled previously. It wasn't just that it was very cold in the north. It was also very quiet, and there was a palpable peacefulness. Around the town, bustling about while speaking in low voices or in silence were orange- and maroon-robed monks and nuns. After securing a tiny room in a hostel along the sloping hillside, I made my way to the Dalai Lama's home.

Many devotees, Westerners and Tibetans alike, were there, engaged in earnest prayer and circumambulating the path outside his residence. Some were walking with prayer beads, and others were making a full bow to the ground with every step. Each was chanting the Tibetan Buddhist mantra, *Om Mane Padme Hum*, which translates as "the jewel in the lotus of the heart." The jewel in this case is a symbol for the spark of divinity hidden within each of our hearts.

The lotus is a symbol found in many Eastern religions. It is a symbol of possibility, a symbol of hope. The lotus seed takes root in the muddy bottom of a pond, then its stalk finds its way through the mud and darkness toward the light, finally breaking through to float on the surface and open its blossom to the sun. The lotus's journey illustrates the journey that many spiritual seekers take from darkness to light. It serves as a reminder that no matter how difficult your life is or has been, what mistakes you may have made, or what someone has done to you, you too have the ability to rise above even the most challenging circumstances and once again open your awareness to the divine.

As I stood in front of his home with a few others, His Holiness emerged through a side door and waved with a joyous smile. He approached us, took my hands in his, and looked into my eyes. He was so present, so powerful, the embodiment of love. I felt, and to this day still feel, blessed by him.

He radiates compassion, kindness, and generosity and shows each of us how it is possible, even in the darkest times, to keep our hearts open and continue the journey toward the goal of love. His humility, strength, and dedication to sharing his message of love, acceptance, and peace, no matter how intense the obstacles or threats, continue to inspire millions of followers worldwide. His life has blossomed like a lotus.

Dark Night

The "dark night of the soul" is a term that was coined by the 16th-century Spanish Carmelite friar John of the Cross. He was a contemporary of Teresa of Avila and supported her efforts to reform the Carmelite order. This work was considered radical, and his fellow monks soon imprisoned him, keeping him in isolation in a tiny cell barely large enough for his body. He was regularly whipped in public, and he was uncertain whether his trials would ever end. His situation triggered his crisis of faith. He felt abandoned by God, whom he calls his "beloved." But John persevered with a continuing conversation to his beloved. He not only won his freedom but also attained spiritual liberation.

The dark night of the soul isn't an experience only reserved for Christians. It can be experienced by anyone. Actually, as we are seeing around the world, it can be a crisis that also affects groups of people who share agreements, fears, beliefs, and social constructs that limit their perspective and connection to the world around them. The crisis is often the impetus behind the dismantling of beliefs and the search for something different. It can awaken people to the beauty and belonging of all of creation.

A dark night of the soul is a sort of existential crisis that gets your attention. Your sense of "I," "me," "mine," and what you believe to be your exclusive place in the world is called into question. The foundation of all that you previously thought to be true about yourself, or your group, is shaken to its very core. You become painfully aware of the areas in which you are not clear, loving, or inclusive. You see the barriers you've erected through the habits and conditions you've attached to that no longer serve you or the greater good. You will be forced to surrender to this expansion, and you will shed outworn parts of your identity and self-image.

Of course, to the ego, this is unbearable. The crisis can rock your stability and leave you feeling deeply uncertain about who you are, why you are here, and what you believe. Yes, this journey can be navigated, but it might terrify you.

Imagine you are standing in a dark hallway, having walked out of a room that represents your past and shut the door behind you. You have no idea where you are because you can't see, so of course you don't know where the hallway leads or if the darkness will ever end. This is the journey "without light or guide, save that which burned in my heart," that John of the Cross wrote about, and that most of us on a spiritual path will also experience to one degree or another.

Call to Love

The dark night of the soul is a call to love *from* love. The difficulties you face during the dark night are unique to you; they are your specific curriculum in this school of life. Your course is designed to awaken you to your full potential and the source of your life. As one of my teachers once asked me, "If this were your only path to God, would you take it?" Most people would say yes, albeit hesitantly.

But some of us won't go on navigating the darkness because the fear of the unknown has proven to be too challenging. Perhaps they feel completely abandoned, alone, and hopeless. The pain, malice, grief, and loss can feel unbearable. It is everyone's sovereign right not to go on. It's completely understandable. However, the suffering will probably continue until you accept it. There is often no way around the experience; you must go *through* it, although it may seem as if the world is against you.

If you are in the midst of a dark night, you might find comfort in knowing that it can be survived and you will thrive. You have everything you need to navigate the challenging terrain ahead.

Stay present and pay attention. The light in your heart will guide you toward wholeness and your full potential.

John of the Cross talked about the light in the heart brightening as that "of noonday." That deepest part of you, that wise and loving consciousness, will guide you through the darkness. It sees beyond the fray with clarity and love and has designed these challenges to call you toward an evolutionary leap.

You've probably heard the saying, "Just when the caterpillar thought the world was over, she became a butterfly." That's the perfect metaphor for the dark night of the soul. In the Buddhist tradition, it is referred to as "falling into the pit of the void." It's the temporary yet life-altering dissolution of the individual self. So, truly, like the caterpillar, life as you knew it is over. If you stay present, clarity will be born from confusion.

Purification

During training at the Meditation Teacher Academy, I let the students know that the journey to expand one's awareness is not for the faint of heart. Anyone who has chosen to take the path toward a deeper connection to the field of love can't help but evolve. In fact, many people establish a meditation practice because they want to better navigate some emotional turmoil or a health issue; then, they inadvertently wake up to much more. The practice of meditation brings deeper connections to yourself and others, enhanced well-being, increased contentment, and expanded awareness; illuminated will be the joy and beauty of the world.

Also illuminated will be the shadowy places and dark corners of your interior: suppressed emotions, repressed memories, false beliefs, grudges, and unexpressed truths. Your personal issues will become magnified and self-defeating behaviors will be revealed. So, too, will be the attachments to and expectations of the way you want people to behave, and the way you want things to be.

Yes, you can dismantle the barriers, undo the habits, and eliminate the conditions that prevent peace and contentment. But first, as these barriers are revealed to you, you have to muster up the courage to admit to them. It can be embarrassing to know you've been living with them, unquestioned and unaddressed until now. But perhaps you didn't even know they were there. In addition to having courage, you'll also need to be compassionate toward yourself.

When you put your gentle attention on the limitations that are revealed to you, you will know whether to delve in through inquiry or to be mindful and simply focus on what new habits you want to establish. You will also need a beginner's mind and the willingness to try something new. Be kind to yourself and remain present as you weather the changes that will inevitably occur in all areas of your life.

Though you might be shaken to the core and would prefer to stay in bed, it's important to go on, to keep up your *sadhana*—a word that in both Tibetan and Sanskrit means an ego-transcending spiritual practice. So whether your practice is prayer, journaling, mindful movement, inquiry, yoga, or meditation, don't abandon it. Your sadhana will support your expanded awareness, keep you grounded, and yoke your attention to its source.

You will also notice your resistance to the changes that are occurring, and you may experience emotional turbulence and unsettling physical sensations. Though extremely disconcerting, you will soon see that your journey is bringing you to a gateway, a chance to awaken to love.

Veils of ignorance can and will fall away, and slowly what blocks the light of your awareness is dissolved. Your individual sense of self begins to merge into the oneness of all things, and in retrospect, you will realize that the field of love conspired and orchestrated every thing, situation, and experience needed to propel you on this evolutionary adventure.

On this spiritual path, there is no ultimate end. The journey *is* the destination. Though it can be painful, it is through these trials and challenges that your heart breaks so wide open that change is inevitable. Even though it doesn't always feel like it, this dark night doesn't happen *to* you, it happens *for* you.

The Odyssey

Some who have lived through a dark night of the soul describe it as a spiritual emergency. Others think of it as the archetypal hero's journey, not unlike Homer's *Odyssey* or Luke Skywalker's evolving character in the movie *Star Wars*. The hero or heroine is called from the ordinary world to adventure and on the journey meets mentors, allies, trials, and enemies. There is inevitably an ordeal that occurs that causes a figurative death. The hero is reborn, transformed with a newfound sense of purpose and perspective, and returns to serve the ordinary world with greater wisdom and mastery.

A dark night can last for an hour, a day, or a span of years. Like birth, death, and even enlightenment, it seems to unfold according to its own timeline. Here's what you don't need as you travel through the darkness: preconceived notions, attachments, and expectations. Instead, along with courage and self-compassion, you need a sense of humor if you can muster one, and to be comfortable with *not knowing*. It's like a trust fall. Ultimately it's easier to let go and allow the journey to take you where it may, surrendering completely to what *is* happening rather than desperately clinging to what you think *should* be happening.

The darkness is an initiation—one that marks a transformation of consciousness and a radical change in perspective. It is analogous to being birthed. As a baby gets pushed through the dark, narrow birth canal, it may seem at times like the process will never end. It can also seem difficult, if not impossible, to endure. And then, suddenly, as if in response to some mysterious culmination, the newborn emerges to a world of love, light, space, sound, touch, and breath—a completely new and expansive reality.

I love the explanation of the dark night of the soul offered by the late David Hawkins, a spiritual teacher who lived in Sedona. In his book *Transcending the Levels of Consciousness*, he suggests this journey is a paradox and that, though seemingly devastating, it's actually a sign of significant spiritual progress. He goes on to say:

> For it is not really the soul . . . but the ego that is in the dark. Some comfort can be obtained by recalling the spiritual dictum that one can only go as high as they have been low, or that Jesus Christ sweat blood in Gethsemane, or that the Buddha reported that he felt as though his bones were being broken and he was being attacked by demons.

Thomas Merton also describes this paradox, saying, "Only when we are able to 'let go' of everything within us, all desire to see, to know, to taste, and to experience the presence of God, do we truly become able to experience that presence."

Bucky

People experience this time of deep inner conflict in different ways. Some scream, some become furious. Others cry endlessly, or fall into deep depression. There are those who succumb to bad habits and dangerous behavior, or even consider suicide. Fortunately, most make it through their dark night to the illumination that awaits them on the other side.

R. Buckminster Fuller, an American engineer, avid futurist, and recognized genius, was best known for innovative building designs such as his patented geodesic dome. His dark night of the soul led him to devote his life to inventing devices that would help humankind and the planet.

Born in 1895 in New England, Bucky, as he was called, learned early on to respect nature. During his family's summer vacations in Maine, he learned to build and maintain boats. He entered Harvard University in 1913, but was expelled twice for not attending classes, so he joined the Navy. While enlisted, he engineered a winch that ships could use to lift airplanes downed in the sea in time to save the lives of the men onboard. This earned him a nomination to attend the U.S. Naval Academy in Annapolis, which he accepted.

Later, he married and fathered a little girl who died from complications of polio and spinal meningitis just before her fourth birthday. Bucky felt responsible for his daughter's death, believing it was caused by the damp and drafty home where they lived. He joined his father-in-law in a construction business that aimed to provide affordable, efficient housing. And while investors were inspired by his genius, the business went bankrupt in 1927.

Bucky was in debt and feeling as if he had let down those who had believed in him when he found out he had a new child on the way. Winter was coming and he began drinking heavily. While taking long walks along the shores of Lake Michigan, he reflected on his family's struggles. One evening, he seriously considered killing himself so his family could benefit from his life insurance policy. But as he walked, something happened. He had what he described as an awakening. According to a biography, Bucky was suddenly lifted several feet above the ground, inside a "sparkling sphere of light," and a voice that spoke directly to him declared:

> You do not have the right to eliminate yourself. You do not belong to you. You belong to the Universe. Your significance will remain forever obscure to you, but you may assume that you are fulfilling your role if you apply yourself to converting your experiences to the highest advantage of others.

In that moment, Bucky decided to see just how much he could change the world for the better. He went into seclusion for two years on a quest to discover the principles that governed the universe so that he could use them to advance the evolution of humanity. He emerged emboldened by the belief that, as society's consciousness evolved, people had the capacity to emerge from the "dark ages"—a time in which people were starving, poorly sheltered, and living out of harmony with the planet—into an incredibly prosperous age. He knew that civilization needed to do more with less, so that all people everywhere could be safe, comfortable, and free. He created designs with this in mind.

Fuller is now regarded as a visionary, and has been called the Leonardo da Vinci of our century. He was awarded 28 U.S. patents for revolutionary modes of transportation, structures, and energy generators, along with 47 honorary degrees. He believed that he and all humankind were part of an interconnected universal oneness. He firmly believed in equalizing wealth between the elite and the working poor, and saw everyone as responsible parties sharing a ride on this "Spaceship Earth," as he called it.

Idea of God

For many of us on a spiritual path, the journey will undoubtedly bring us face-to-face with our worst fears and our most crippling misconceptions about ourselves and about life itself. The ego is our most tenacious adversary of all. It's the ego that insists that our beliefs about ourselves are true, even when those beliefs are negative or destructive. Our egos falsely convince us that trusting our own thoughts without question will allow us to remain in control of our experiences. (When you really examine it, the reality is that we can't control much in our lives, except where we focus our attention and how we choose to behave.)

Our identity becomes linked with the roles, conditions, labels, and status symbols that we believe define us: "I am a mother." "I'm a millionaire." "I am a failure." Our ego's sole purpose is to maintain and protect all notions of "I," "me," and "mine." To discover our true nature, we must—by definition—dismantle this self-image.

Through meditation and mindfulness, we transcend our sense of individuality and recognize that we are far more than just the labels we assign to ourselves. As a result, an epic battle begins deep within the psyche: the ego, concerned with preserving individuality, strives to maintain control and avoid surrender, while the soul in its universal wisdom relinquishes control and returns to the source it came from.

When conditions in our external world break down, we turn to ego ideals, beliefs, philosophies—such as "I'm strong," "I can handle this," or "at least I have my health"—that nourish our internal sense of self. But when these also break down, we are left with no choice but to surrender completely, whether to God, to nature, or to the field of love that animates all of life.

When his wife died of cancer, Irish writer C. S. Lewis, best known for his children's series The Chronicles of Narnia, wrote his thoughts in the book *A Grief Observed.* "Nothing less will shake a man—or at any rate a man like me—out of his merely verbal thinking and his merely notional beliefs. He has to be knocked silly before he comes to his senses." He *was* knocked silly, and came to realize the reality he had known was "iconoclastic," and he wanted to transcend the icons to have the direct experience of life. He wanted to realize "not my *idea* of God, but God" (italics mine).

A dark night of the soul doesn't happen because there's something wrong with you. Consider instead that it occurs because from the deeper, spiritual perspective, something is going very, very right. I believe that this was the case for Byron Katie. The difficulties that she encountered as a child persisted well into adulthood: she became an alcoholic, developed an eating disorder, and spent most of her days in bed, afraid to go out in public. She describes the experience:

> Nothing felt good, nothing made me happy, nothing brought me peace. In the end I was obese and starving. . . . I was in so much pain and the pills weren't working. I was insane, a dead woman still breathing.

Katie was suffering so much that her husband checked her into a halfway house, hoping to find relief. During her dark night, her regard for herself was so low that she didn't even feel worthy enough to sleep on the bed, so she slept on the floor.

One winter morning in 1986, Katie woke up to reality and experienced an expanded, loving awareness—what Zen Buddhists would call kensho or satori, an awakening. She awakened to the field of love. She shared, "There is only love. . . . There is no time . . . Unlearning is everything."

Katie said that up until that moment, her conditioned mind and its habit of believing the horrible thoughts she had about herself and her family had created massive amounts of stress and suffering. When she believed her thoughts, she suffered, but when she questioned the validity of them, she was free. She believes this same freedom is available to every human being:

> Freedom is as simple as that. I found that suffering is optional. I found a joy within me that has never disappeared, not for a single moment. That joy is in everyone, always.

Recall

John of the Cross's poem was written after he experienced his dark night, so he had the benefit of looking back and seeing it from a new perspective. That's probably why he can refer to the dark night as "the happy night" and the "night more lovely than the dawn." He surely wasn't feeling that way when he was suffering through it. But he did make it through, and when he reflected on his trials and despair, he saw them through the eyes of love, through the eyes of his beloved.

The same can be true for us. When we look back at our worst times, those times that took us to our knees, broke our hearts, and made us feel so desperately alone and scared, our trials now seem perfectly designed for us. Though at times the pain and hurt can still present themselves, the resulting gifts and lessons learned are so great that the pain pales in comparison.

In the shamanic tradition there's a practice called recapitulation. Shamans use the process throughout their lives to purify and reclaim their energy. Others use it as a natural means of processing

a traumatic memory, by seeing it with a new witnessing awareness and reclaiming whatever energy they've unconsciously lost
over it. I first practiced it after reading about it in one of Carlos
Castaneda's books about his shamanic teacher, don Juan, a Yaqui
Indian from Mexico.

The practice of recapitulation (think "recap") consists of purposely recalling one of your life's experiences down to every detail
and every moment. You witness everything that occurred with a
wise and loving perspective. In this way, you'll be able to integrate
the entire experience.

I must warn you, however, not to do the following recapitulation exercise if you are currently in the middle of a dark night.
You won't have the perspective you need to look back right now,
especially if everything is just too confusing or painful. Instead, I
would encourage you to practice the Breath-Awareness Meditation
in Chapter 2 or the Loving Kindness Meditation in Chapter 5.

The kind thing to do during a crisis is to take care of yourself as
you navigate the rough terrain. You also need to be reminded that
you are lovable. Here's something the Buddha has been quoted as
saying that I have always found helpful:

> You can search throughout the entire universe for
> someone who is more deserving of your love and affection
> than you are yourself, and that person is not to be found
> anywhere. You yourself, as much as anybody in the entire
> universe, deserve your love and affection.

Recapitulation*

This ancient technique is holistic, as it integrates your experience on spiritual, mental, energetic, and physical levels. You can recapitulate an experience a few different times in order to completely integrate it.

Before you begin, write down a list of life events that were terribly difficult to bear. Choose events that happened at least two years ago; don't attempt this exercise with a difficult situation that you are currently going through. (Most of us need distance to gain the perspective needed for the following exercise.)

Read through the following instructions. Review them again before you begin. It's natural not to remember each and every step, but as time goes by, this practice can become second nature.

- Choose one specific event from your list to work on now. (You can work through your list, selecting a different situation for each session.)

- Set aside at least 15 minutes when you will be free of disturbances. Keep track of the time with a clock, watch, or meditation timer.

- Find a space where you can be alone and feel safe. You can tuck yourself away in a closet where you'll feel cocooned or wrap yourself in a heavy quilt or blanket.

- Keep distractions to a minimum. Put a "Do Not Disturb" sign on your door, turn off your cell phone, turn off your TV, and turn off music.

- If you like, you can turn down the lights and light a candle.

*This practice is not intended as a substitution for treatment by a health care professional. Seek a qualified counselor if you are experiencing significant problems functioning in your everyday life or are suffering from overwhelming emotions or a mental disturbance. If you are currently in treatment or in therapy, please consult your therapist, psychiatrist, or mental-health professional before you do this exercise.

Close your eyes and relax your body. Let go of any obvious tension as you settle into your seat and find comfort.

Begin breathing deeply. Inhale slowly and deeply through your nostrils, visualizing your body expanding in 360 degrees. Exhale slowly and fully through your nostrils. Do this three times, then return to your breath's natural rhythm and depth.

Bring the event in as much detail as possible to your mind's eye. Recall the place, the season, the time of day, the people around you, the sounds you heard, everything. During this recall, slowly turn your head to the left while exhaling, then slowly turn your head to center and to the right while inhaling. (Exhaling from right to left releases energy that is not yours. Inhaling from left to right draws in the energy you lost at the scene.)

Continue the recall while keeping the rhythm of sweeping your head back and forth, exhaling from right to left, inhaling from left to right. Don't force this; just allow it to be easy.

Notice what emotions of yours were present and, if you weren't alone, what emotions of others were present. Stay aware as you observe.

Recall as much as you can: what people said, what you did, what you felt, what you wore, what you ate, everything. Watch intently. Keep breathing, and keep your body relaxed.

Don't worry if you lose focus; simply return your attention to the scene until time is up. Allow whatever you feel to arise in response to recalling the event. Don't leave yourself; don't force a feeling. This is not a time for philosophies or repression. Be patient.

At the end of your time, or when you feel as if you've recalled what you can, stop the exercise.

Continue to sit in the stillness for a few minutes. Take your time coming out of the meditation, breathing deeply and stretching into the space around you.

Open your eyes slowly—first with a downward gaze, then opening them up all the way.

Once you open your eyes, you might feel energized and ready to go—or you might need to stay still for a little bit because you feel light-headed. You may even want to go take a nap because you feel sleepy. Whatever you feel is normal. Be kind and loving toward yourself by honoring your body and the sensations you are experiencing.

After the recapitulation, I find it comforting to go for a walk in nature and feel my place in the world. Some people might take some time to themselves with a long, leisurely bath.

Once you feel fully aware of the present moment, you can then ask yourself the following questions:

- *What gifts did I receive from this situation?*

- *How did it transform me or alter my perspective?*

- *What matters now?*

Every dark night comes to an end eventually, and it can certainly seem darkest before the dawn. When you heed its call and commit to the journey, and learn what it has to teach you, you emerge completely transformed.

In the Bible, Jesus says, "The one who will lose their life will save it." You emerge from the dark night of the soul with your ego subdued and with less attachment to positions, possessions, cultural conditioning, and adopted social norms. As you die to your old way of looking at yourself and life, a new perspective is born, one that calls you to live more fully, more powerfully, and more in harmony with all other beings on this planet. You truly realize that you are an expression of the powerful force field of love.

Chapter 7

Walking a New Path

I might pursue some path, however solitary and narrow and crooked, in which I could walk with love and reverence.

—HENRY DAVID THOREAU

Having emerged—scathed or unscathed—from your dark night of the soul, you are, in a sense, reborn into the world. As limiting thoughts, beliefs, and notions about yourself gradually loosen their grip on you, a resurgence of vitality, clarity, and sense of purpose will emerge. You become more mindful of patterns of behavior that were once automatic and unquestioned. You find yourself in a new world full of infinite possibilities and opportunities.

It's like the heroine's journey depicted in one of my favorite movies, *The Wizard of Oz*. Dorothy, an orphan, takes a journey somewhere over the rainbow, from Kansas—a colorless land of storms and tornadoes where she's saddled with her habits of people-pleasing and powerlessness—to Oz, a vibrant, sparkling, magical scene where she develops courage and clarity. It's a mythic adventure toward self-awareness, transformation, and even perhaps enlightenment.

No Place Like Home

As 12-year-old Dorothy arrives in the Land of Oz, she is met by Glinda the Good Witch, a wise, kind, and loving guide. Glinda tells Dorothy that there is a path to everything she desires, and that she has the ability to find it. She adorns Dorothy with a pair of ruby red shoes for her journey and tells her to "start at the beginning." Dorothy follows the road of bright yellow bricks with her little dog, Toto, and begins her quest down the unwinding spiral path into the unknown.

Dorothy soon encounters three characters who quickly become friends and join the path with her. Although the tale seems at first to be an outward journey, it's actually an inward journey. They navigate through the experiences of fear and courage, hatred and love, doubt and faith.

When the friends arrive in the Emerald City, they hope to receive wisdom, courage, and heart from the great Wizard of Oz. However, after great struggles and adventures, the Wizard is exposed as a fake, and the friends realize that they can't get what they are looking for from him. Instead, they each discover that everything they ever needed is already inside them. When Dorothy returns to her home in Kansas, she sees the familiar landscape through new eyes and with an open heart. Home is where her heart is; she simply needed to recognize it.

There are so many choices you can make, so much you will awaken to that perhaps you hadn't been aware of before, and all that is required to realize the fullness of it is to journey with attention. With awareness, the signs and wonders will be clear. You'll be guided in the perfect direction to actualize your potential and awaken your true power. Everything you have been looking for to feel safe will arise to meet the call of your heart, orchestrated by the field of love. Home is your true Self, and that's where you'll return after all this journeying. You, too, will see it as if for the first time!

Two Paths

There are two ways to do everything. Thanks to recent research in neuroscience, we now understand that, in each moment, all human beings are choosing between two distinct and opposite pathways—the *default neural network* and the *direct experience neural network*—when interacting with the world. In other words, when you perform your daily activities such as driving, eating, working, and being with friends and family, you can engage your full awareness, or you can just go through the motions.

The default neural network is the brain's autopilot. It's operating when not much else is happening, or when you are performing a rote activity that demands very little attention, such as driving or taking a shower. While you are performing the task, it's as if your brain is running another program in the background, one that is taking most of its attention.

While this mode can be helpful for tasks like planning, recollection, and critical thinking, it's detrimental to the cultivation of attention and to being fully engaged in the goings-on in your life. This mode also creates habitual thinking, because when you think, do, and conclude the same things (much of which is unconscious) over and over again, day after day, deep grooves—like well-traveled roads—are worn into the brain's neural pathways.

The direct experience neural network, on the other hand, is the one that engages your full attention. When you're in direct experience mode, everything you encounter becomes richer and more meaningful. With your nonjudgmental attention at the helm, you can act on purpose, mindfully attending to what you're doing so you can savor the moments and free yourself from the background thinking or habits of mind that distract you. The direct experience network is needed for you to live and act with "love and reverence," as Thoreau longed to do.

Beginner's Mind

Imagine yourself going out for the evening to watch a live performance by an orchestra or your favorite band. If you arrive and your brain is stuck in default mode, your perception of the experience will be limited only to your thoughts *about* the event—such as critiquing the venue, thinking about how much the tickets cost, evaluating your seats' position, or comparing this performance with those you've heard previously. Your brain naturally wants to identify and catalog what is happening. It names, labels, separates, compares, and often judges everyone and everything.

In contrast, if you arrive at the concert with your brain's direct experience network activated, you are fully present to the nuances of the music. You feel the excitement as each moment unfolds. Your senses are engaged, and your attention is captivated.

To give you an example of how radically different our perception is when we're using the direct experience network, I'd like to tell you about the cardinal that lives beside my house. The first thing in the morning, on almost every morning, I hear him before I see him. He sits and sings, hidden among the branches of the tree outside my open window. As the sun rises it illuminates him, his red feathers and orange beak contrasting with the deep green needles and the dark brown bark of the piñon tree. His activity alternates between lifting his wings, pruning his feathers, and singing very loudly.

That's the best I can do to describe the scene. Maybe you know what I am talking about because you "know" what a cardinal looks like, or perhaps you can picture what I am saying. However, you will never have the direct experience of that moment or that cardinal, but instead only the experience of the story I told about him.

I could look out the window and say, "Oh, it's that bird again." Or I could hear it and think, *I know it's that bird*, and go into the other room. And if I do, I would miss the opportunity to be present to the beauty and wonder of the moment. I could allow my idea of "bird" to diminish the reality. Instead, I make the choice to have the direct experience of the moment. I hear his call, and I look and listen without my predetermined idea of "bird" or "cardinal." I see his beauty and hear his glorious sounds and there is no separation between him and me.

The internal dialogue that insists *I know this band* or *I've seen that bird* or *I've done that before* actually shuts down the direct experience network and instead puts up a false screen between you and it, a screen full of labels and ideas. This can become a habitual way to respond to people and the environment. It's like seeing life through the lens of your cell phone camera. It's obvious you've been to these places and had these experiences, as there are photos to prove it. But did you truly see and appreciate who you were with and where you have been? If not, the great news is that you can change the way you interact with life. All you need is the desire to change it.

In Zen practice, this state of being present and engaged is known as having a "beginner's mind" and is also the practice of "not knowing." As the beginner's mind is cultivated through meditation and mindful living, it creates new neural pathways, making it possible for you to forego your preconceived notions. You soon drop your ideas about how a certain person, group of people, or thing "should" be; more natural, intimate, in-the-moment connection between you and all of those around you emerges instead. You experience your life directly, rather than through the default filter of your judgments and preconceptions. It's a beautiful way to live.

Savor the Moments

Without the obstructive overlay of narrative thoughts, your senses are enlivened and your awareness is clear. With a beginner's mind and an open heart, what might have been perceived as an ordinary sensory experience becomes extraordinary. As you savor what is unfolding before you, a sublime, expansive, and mystical world will reveal itself.

I imagine you have experienced some expansive and transcendent moments that are indelibly imprinted in your mind. Here are a few I've experienced and will attempt to put into words, although by their very nature, direct experiences are difficult to explain. It's like trying to describe a sunrise, a bird's song, or a juicy peach. Words will never, ever capture their essence.

I was in school in France for the summer. One beautifully warm night I attended an outdoor concert in Paris. The dark night and the twinkling lights of the city were the perfect backdrop. When I heard the clear notes from Miles Davis's trumpet pierce the silence, my body tingled with bliss and tears welled up in my eyes. I can hear it and feel it now. I was in love with sound, and the sound was loving me, too.

Years later, another transcendent moment happened for me on a backpacking trip along the Long Trail in Vermont's Green Mountains. I had been hiking for over an hour and was deep in the woods of majestic pines. It was a crisp, early morning. I felt the presence of the community of trees that surrounded me. I stopped and joined them in their stillness and presence. We were nature's kingdom. In that moment, the trees and I were in love.

During my travels in Pakistan I had camped at a long-forgotten British hill station in the Karakoram Mountains. One day, as the sun broke the horizon, I woke up to the aroma of dung fires in a village in the valley far below. Somehow, as I peeked out of my tiny tent in this far-off place, I felt like I was home, loved, and safe in a perfect world.

Lover and Beloved

We all go through life as the observer, seeing life through our own lens. You have been the architect of your beliefs, which have determined to a large extent how life is perceived and processed by you. Through your lens, you watch, listen, are present for, and engage with people, places, and things. And if you have gotten this far in the book, you've probably been paying more attention to everything, and even polished the lens through which you see life.

But have you ever considered that you are not just the observer, but also that which is being observed?

What if you are not solely the subject, but also simultaneously the object of attention? Thomas Jefferson once wrote, "Whenever you do a thing, act as if all the world were watching." Consider the fact that every single thing surrounding you in this moment is also an expression of consciousness. It knows you are there. You are being seen, listened to, and paid attention to. Everything around you is tuned in to you and is conscious of you. The tree, the desk, your houseplant—everything. Just because something doesn't have eyes doesn't mean it isn't aware of you and what your heart wants. (Remember those houseplants that knew where the scientists were, and even their states of mind?)

The field of love expresses itself through each and every thing. It is unseen, conscious, intelligent, and orchestrating everything. It is responsible for coincidences, for miracles, and for your true heart's desires made manifest. The web of loving intelligence is at the source of it all. And it is a web of love that lovingly responds to you in wonder-filled ways. The fusion between lover and beloved occurs in these magical moments.

If you know yourself as the beloved and everything around you loves you, make a conscious effort to be receptive and open to receiving everything—whether it is a beautiful moment, an inspirational idea, or a sign to go in a different direction. One way to actualize the experience of life loving you is to practice being seen, being heard, being touched, and being loved by everything. You can do this easily by going out into nature and sitting on a grassy knoll or taking a walk through an open landscape. If you can, make it a point to spend at least an hour every day in nature, and be seen by nature. Try it without your electronic devices, and you may experience for yourself just how much life loves you.

Being in nature offers physical benefits as well, including normalizing your blood pressure, increasing your immunity, and balancing your hormones. It also helps to alleviate depression and anxiety. You'll experience more positive emotions and more serenity and will recover more quickly from stress. When you go analog, you'll even become more creative, present, and resilient—just like nature herself.

Signs and Wonders

You have learned, and hopefully have practiced, the meditations and exercises offered in this book. The meditations, especially the mantra practices, will give you direct experience of the field of love. The universe, and everything within its realm, is an expression of this field of love. When you transcend in meditation and dive into this field again and again, you'll have a direct experience of it. And as you do, conditioning is dissolved and your awareness expands. The *idea* of this field becomes a reality both in and out of meditation.

Your attention is an extension of this conscious field. It is the instrument through which the field interacts with itself as it lives through you. Your attention is very powerful, because the field of love is omnipotent. Your attention is naturally very present, because the field is omnipresent. Your attention is timeless, just as the field is eternal. Your attention is intelligent, as the field is wise.

Your desires are the desires of the field as well, simply because you are an individual expression of the field. When you tune in to your heart and tune out distractions—in other words, when you focus your intentional attention—your true desires will be revealed to you. The beautiful thing is that these desires are not accidental. In fact, they are part of the field's infinite organizing power and guidance on your path.

When you are present and your mind is clear, you'll recognize that there are a myriad of signs and wonders pointing you in the direction of fulfillment. Remember, *what you are seeking is seeking you*. If you have faith in this, then every heart's desire you acknowledge, every idea that stirs your curiosity, every person you engage with, and every experience you are mindful of can and will offer you the clues you need to move you toward the path of your greatest personal fulfillment and your highest contribution to others.

Your path will be illuminated, perhaps not by yellow bricks, but it will light up for you, one step at a time. You don't have to see the top of the mountain in order to climb it. Instead, you'll need to start at the beginning, as Glinda said, and bring your beginner's mind. You'll need an open heart. You'll need to be brave. And you'll need to pay attention to the signs that appear along the way.

Quantum Healing

Have you ever been spontaneously led toward the next stop on your journey? It's almost as if there is a benevolent unseen hand nudging you in the right direction. Perhaps it was the result of a conversation with a stranger who provided the answer to a question without your ever having to ask, an article you read about someone you just had to meet, or a detour in the course of your journey—on a particular career path, for instance—that took you on a road to an opportunity better than anything you had envisioned for yourself. You can be assured that all this is an orchestration of the field. It loves you so much that it will make all your dreams come true if you are clear, present, and attentive.

This happened to me. After returning from my nine-month bicycling trip through Europe and the Middle East, I landed a job in Washington, D.C., selling real estate. Initially, I found the work interesting, and in a relatively short time, I attained a new level of material and professional success. I had a great group of friends, and even purchased my first home. But a year and a half into it, I was starting to wonder what was next for me. I had already accomplished quite a bit for a 27-year-old, but I was ready for something more. *What is next?* I asked myself. I believe that question prompted the field of love to orchestrate my personal journey to Oz.

The answer came a few mornings later as I was reading the book review section of *The Washington Post*. I felt a wave of excitement about a book on a subject I had never heard of before: ayurveda. I was intrigued by all the methods that were described to cultivate mind-body health: herbs, aroma oils, meditation, yoga, sound therapy, and even color therapy.

The book was by Deepak Chopra, and though you might know who he is now, back in 1989, his name was not on the tip of everyone's tongue. As I read the review, I felt what seemed like an electrical current running through my body. I went to the local bookstore in Georgetown and saw not one but two books by Chopra, *Perfect Health* and *Quantum Healing*. I held each one, and for some reason, I put them down again. Perhaps on some level I knew my life was about to change and I was scared of what was to come. Whatever it was, it prompted me to leave the store empty-handed.

The Turnaround

Soon, I had forgotten about the book. And when I was invited on a trip to Florida to help do some interior decorating for the *Barefoot Contessa*—a yacht recently purchased by the company I worked for—I jumped at the chance.

When we arrived, I was comforted by the ocean's endless movement. It was my first time on a ship of that size and my first time sleeping on one, too. It felt as if an invisible loving force was rocking me. A deep sense of peace was seeping into my bones. Three days later, when everyone else was leaving to go back to D.C., I really didn't want to join them. I made the decision to stay on the boat alone, though I didn't know for how long.

The first night I tossed and turned in my cabin. I couldn't sleep. I felt an overwhelming sadness, and I soon was sobbing and wailing into my pillow. I had no sense of what this grief was about. It went on all night. I felt desperate. Was it going to end?

Just before the sun came up, I went to the captain's wheelhouse, where I found a phone book. I plugged the phone cord into the outlet on the dock and did something I'd never done before: I called a prayer service: dial-a-prayer. I was grateful for the minister who had recorded these prayers for people just like me. I cried and cried as I listened to each one, and then, finally, as the sky brightened, I was calm enough to fall sleep.

I spent the next day crying on and off while washing down the boat's decks. As the afternoon waned, I left the boat to walk on the beach. It was a magical time of day, with the sun setting over the Intracoastal Waterway. As I walked along in the sand, the low-hanging clouds were awash with the brilliant fuchsia and orange light of the setting sun. Their beauty took my breath away. I felt a deep sense of peace and belonging. I was going to be all right. I was being loved by this world.

My tears stopped and I felt a strong urge to turn around and walk back the other way. Whether it was the clouds or my intuition, I'll never know, but I did turn around, and found what would be the biggest turning point in my life at that time.

As I walked, two colorful sails caught my eye. Now, sails at the beach are a common enough sight, but I was drawn toward these two moving in perfect synchrony in the beach's parking lot. When I got close enough, I saw they were in fact windsurf sails attached to skateboards, each being navigated in the gentle breeze by one of two young men.

I watched the sails for a while, mesmerized by the motion and the backdrop of the setting sun. Then, my attention was drawn to one of men, and I heard, or thought I heard, the word *him*.

"Him"? I asked myself. *What does that mean?*

I turned my back to the windsurfers and sat on the seawall, directing my gaze once again toward the ocean and appreciating the light of the setting sun playing on the clouds and the waves. That's when one of the young men, the one with the blond ponytail, stopped skating and sat down next to me on the wall. He was sipping a Coke and wearing green lizard-skin boat shoes. We spoke for a while, then he asked if I'd like to share a pizza with him. I agreed and suggested that he get the pizza and bring it on the boat so we could eat there. I gave him directions to the marina nearby.

As we ate, I learned that this man, Joe, was a computer programmer. He found out I was a real-estate agent. He asked what I really would like to do. I responded by telling him that I'd like to get involved with ayurveda. My response surprised me because I hadn't thought about it since that moment in the bookstore. I don't even know if I pronounced it correctly. But it didn't matter; his eyes lit up. He knew what I was talking about. He excitedly told me that he'd been raised in a family in which everyone meditated and practiced ayurvedic principles. We stayed up almost all night talking about ayurveda, meditation, mind-body health, and the directions of our lives.

We continued to see each other over the next few days. It was obvious we really enjoyed each other's company. He told me that if I wanted to be his girlfriend, I'd have to learn to meditate. So when I returned to Washington, D.C., I did, and that first meditation was as soothing as that moment on the beach had been.

There was something happening here; I felt love like I had never felt. I read the book *Perfect Health* and it affirmed that I truly wanted to experience every treatment, explore each modality of healing, and learn more about all I had read about. In the back of the book, there was a number to call for more information, and I called it. I asked the director, a man named Mr. Pleasant, if they needed help of any sort. They certainly did, and a month later, I was on my way to Massachusetts—to the center where Deepak Chopra worked. I left my home and my job in D.C. to follow my yellow brick road.

Who am I? Why am I here? What's next? Perhaps those questions called forth the signs and wonders that pointed out my path to the life I'm living today. My curiosity and sensitivity were what preceded the dark night and led me through it. Maybe it started with reading the book review, and went on to include my piqued interest in ayurveda, the decision to stay a few more days on the boat, the prompt to turn around on the beach, my attraction to the sails, and my dinner with Joe.

As I learned to be present, follow my heart, and heed my inner knowing, the perfect path began to unfold before me. I am where

I'm meant to be, doing the work that I was born to do. And it's all because life loves me. As it does you. I believe that the universal field of intelligence has the ultimate overview. It organizes possibilities that our human minds cannot contrive. And when we are paying attention, it wakes us up to guide us—step-by-step—to the best moments of our lives.

Presence Meditation

This practice will help you be more attentive to your inner landscape and train your attention to be right here, right now.

Read through the following instructions. Review them again before your practice. It's natural not to remember each and every step, but as time goes by, it will become second nature.

- Before you start, determine how long you'll be doing this practice. Be deliberate and stick to it. Anywhere from 10 to 20 minutes is fine, and plan for an integration period of a few minutes afterward. Keep track of the time with a clock, watch, or meditation timer.

- Keep distractions to a minimum. Put a "Do Not Disturb" sign on your door, turn off your cell phone, turn off your TV, and turn off music. Silence will allow you to be more present to what is happening.

- Let go of expectations, and don't judge your experience. Welcome everything, resist nothing. Be kind to yourself. If your thoughts wander and interrupt the experience, simply begin again by refocusing on the instructions. Don't try to have a certain experience. Whatever experience you have is the right one for you at this time.

Give yourself a few slow, deep breaths in and out through your nose. Gather yourself. You, your body, your breath, and your life are all right here, right now.

Let your breath be natural as your body relaxes.

Silently ask yourself: Where is here?

Instead of listening to the interpretations offered by your mind, use your senses to have a direct experience of here. Let go of memory and names of things.

Close your eyes and shift your attention to listening. Simply listen to the sounds around you without identifying what they are or what is creating them.

Notice how you receive sound. Notice faraway sounds with your bare attention.

Notice as sounds emerge from the silence and stay awhile. Notice as they dissipate into the silence. Continue to listen like this for a few moments.

Bring your attention to those sounds that are closer, or even inside you.

There's no need to identify the source of the sounds or label the sounds. Instead, notice them arising from wherever they are. You can close your eyes to do this for a few minutes.

Now, with your eyes open, notice what you can see of your body. Without labels, notice the space in which your body exists.

Close your eyes and feel the places where your body meets objects in space: a chair, a cushion, the floor, etc. Feel where your body begins and ends.

Notice sensations of comfort and discomfort. Let them arise without judgment or wishing things were different. Don't label any feelings that arise or tell yourself stories about why this or that is occurring.

Notice the varying temperatures throughout your body, coolness and warmth. Notice heaviness and lightness. Notice dryness and dampness. Notice the air on your skin, the sensation of clothes against your body.

Abandon preferences; simply be in the experience.

With your eyes closed, expand your attention to your whole body. Notice the sensations of being alive, in whatever way your attention is drawn.

Welcome the sensation of your heart beating, your pulse, and any tingling you might feel. Notice your body's response to breath. Feel what is here. Explore your body's sensations for a while.

Now open your eyes and notice your surroundings. See who and what is in your space.

See what lies in the distance and what is closer to you. Notice what objects take up space in your room. Notice how your bare attention "touches" each item.

Abandon judgments and preferences, and simply look. No labels are needed.

Now notice the space between things. Notice the spaces between you and that which you see, and the spaces between all that's here.

See the shadows. Notice the light. Notice where light meets shadows.

Notice the array of colors and shapes that surround you. See the patterns and textures, all without naming them.

Simply see. Welcome everything.

Notice what is moving. See what is still.

Now notice the stillness of you. Notice the movement of you, inside and outside. Witness the sensations.

Now bring your attention to your breath as it naturally moves in and out of your nostrils. Don't try to control or change it. Feel the movement as your body gives and receives breath. Notice the pauses between each breath.

Welcome all sensations of the breath. Feel them without judgment or trying to control anything. Your breath anchors you right here. Give yourself time to do this. Let the sensation of the inhalations and exhalations charm your attention.

When the period comes to an end, keep your eyes closed for a few minutes. Become more alert to the one who is coming out of meditation. Become alert to the one who is hearing the sounds outside of you.

Give yourself some deeper breaths, and stretch into the space around you. Eventually, when you feel ready, slowly open your eyes all the way. Take your time before engaging in activity.

When you are resting in the stream of your open, natural awareness, the urge to control, coerce, label, judge, or manipulate life dissipates. Instead, you surrender to life's flow. You are empowered by the realization that you're not a separate entity, but rather a direct extension of the field of love that expresses itself as the manifest universe. And you are an integral part of its expression.

As the habits of your wandering mind lessen, you attune to your inner world and your true nature. You become more aware of your awareness and its unconditioned, loving natural state. You awaken to the support of all that is around you and realize the unlimited potential of the field.

Life is unfolding for you right here, right in this moment. Now is the time to live your beautiful life.

Chapter 8

Love in Action

*The one hope for the future lies, I believe, in Sacred Activism—
the fusion of the deepest spiritual knowledge and passion with
clear, wise, radical action in all the arenas of the world, inner
and outer. We have very little time in which to awaken and
transform ourselves, to be able to preserve the planet, and to heal
the divisions between the powerful and the powerless. Let us go
forward now with firm resolve and profound dedication.*

—ANDREW HARVEY

What were you born to do? Why are you here? Sooner or later, these questions arise in everyone's heart. It can take time for the answers to be revealed, but you can do your part so that when they do arise, you won't miss them. Remain present and alert to each moment.

The answers and resources you seek reveal themselves in the present moment, and when they do, you will know it, because you will feel it in every cell of your body. The field of love will naturally propel you toward your *swadharma*, a Sanskrit word that means "your own life purpose according to your nature."

Along the way to this important discovery, you might have gotten sidetracked. Perhaps you took on a role that doesn't quite fit or signed up for so many responsibilities that you've been too busy to even ask yourself if this is really the right path for you. Some of us have been so otherwise occupied in our pursuit of money, prestige, or approval that we can be blinded from our true purpose because we weren't paying attention.

Luckily, if you are not on the path to actualizing your purpose, your body and soul will let you know. Life will let you know. It wants the best for you. It wants you to live as love in action. You might feel very restless, anxious, or even depressed if this is the case. It's as if your life doesn't seem quite right or you just don't fit. This restlessness and discomfort will linger until you find your path or make progress toward it, no matter how many years have passed.

Living your swadharma is not only evolutionary for you but also beneficial for the entire world. Whether you are aware of it or not, you have been selected to play a particular role—a role vital for the awakening and evolution of life on this planet. Whether you are here to express a particular creative talent, advocate for a cause, or be the very best parent or caregiver you can be, you have a part to play. You matter. And when you are ready to roll, all the resources you need to support you in easily actualizing your purpose will make their way to you.

You've Been Selected

Whatever contribution you are called to deliver, it is a relationship between you and creativity. Your responsibility is to fall in love with it. Give up the idea that you need to generate it; instead, let it move through you, and receive the direction, inspiration, and flow.

Here's what happens: A creative impulse arises from the field in order to be made manifest. It circles the globe looking for the perfect host or hostess to help make the impulse a reality, one who can align with the project and be inspired to let it happen. Then, once the perfect person or persons respond to the idea with a resounding, energetic yes, the field conspires and organizes the provision of resources and support for its creation.

To be selected, it can be helpful to acknowledge the gifts you've cultivated or been born with and humbly recognize that you are uniquely suited to give them. Then, when you have been awakened to the call to offer them to the world, say *yes*. The field of love will do the rest. It will provide you with the intellect, wisdom, vitality, skill, resources, and opportunities you need. Love speaks through your voice, radiates through your presence, and is expressed through your compassion, creativity, and actions. You are love in action.

My dear friend and mentor, the late Debbie Ford, described her creative process as one of simply "taking dictation." While writing, designing an internal process, or speaking to an audience about cultivating self-love, she would first become still and what she called "profoundly related"—with her source and with whatever or whomever happened to be the object of her attention in that moment. Then she'd allow herself to become a receptionist for whatever aspect of infinite intelligence came to her wanting to be shared. She was present to the field of love that lived and moved through her.

In her third book, *The Secret of the Shadow*, she wrote: "Each one of us is here to contribute a very special piece of the Divine puzzle—one that no one else can provide." Debbie's unique contribution was to help people make peace with their "shadow." Your shadow is any or all the aspects of yourself that you deem bad or unworthy, feel ashamed of, or are compelled to hide. And though Debbie passed away a couple of years ago from cancer, her legacy lives on in her books, seminars, and the coaching institute that continues to make an enormous difference in the lives of millions of people who will never meet her.

Heroes and Heroines

The field of love is waiting for you. It beckons you to awaken to it so it can express itself through you. The many men and women who have heeded this call—in whatever form or language they received it—become your heroes and heroines. These luminaries have lived in every era of human history. They come forth as peacemakers, mystics, scientists, religious and political leaders, social reformers, environmentalists, artists, philosophers, and activists because they have important work to do.

In the words of Kahlil Gibran, the Lebanese poet and author of *The Prophet*, their "work is love made visible." Whatever type of work they are called to, these agents of change come forth to reveal and awaken humanity's relationship to the field of love. They live a life of love in action. And you can be one of them. You don't have to be in a particular profession, have a certain amount of education, look a specific way, or have a lot of money to make a difference either. You can express this field of love through anything you are called to do.

My friend Andrea Smith, who has a gallery in Sedona, was "called" to a life of love in action while living and teaching in Detroit in 1969. As a young wife, she'd watch the reports of the war in Vietnam on TV and hold her very pregnant belly and wonder what would happen to her baby if it were born a boy. Weeks later, holding her baby boy, she made the connection between the deaths of all the young boys in the war and her precious newborn. It was then that she vowed to never let her child go to war or participate in killing anyone. She hated war. She prayed for help. A few years later she had a baby girl, and again she prayed for help. This time, she clearly heard a response, which was: "If you want peace on Earth, find the peace within."

It was then that she stopped teaching school and devoted herself to her art. She also made her spirituality a priority, reading books on health, healing, and self-awareness. She read a passage that struck her: "You will never change anything by hating it. Instead, you have to love whatever the opposite of it seems to be." In that moment, she determined that she would have to stop hating war and start loving peace.

From then on, every painting she created was motivated by peace. She has been painting professionally since 1978, and over 4,000 paintings have "come though" her as expressions of love, gratitude, or peace. She says she doesn't have to do anything other than put the brush in her hand, get out of the way, and let the paintings flow effortlessly onto the canvas. Andrea says, "I realize when I do what I love, everything else falls into place." She continues to dedicate her unique talents toward the ending of war and the realization of peace.

Julia Butterfly Hill is a heroine to many, as she is to me. In 1997, she left her home in Arkansas and traveled to California. A year earlier, she had been in a serious car accident caused by a drunk driver and was looking for healing. In California, she learned about local efforts to save old-growth forests from Pacific Lumber, a company that had been routinely clear-cutting the forest in the area. Julia immediately awakened to the call. She knew she would take whatever action she could to save the trees from this ongoing threat, even in the face of dangerous and strong opposition.

When she went into the forest, she felt an instant connection to the redwood trees. And though she had no previous experience, she became a tree sitter. She settled under the canopy of a 1,000-year-old redwood tree she called Luna. Her home was a 6-by-6-foot platform 180 feet above the ground—the height of an 18-story building. There, she spent 738 days sleeping, eating, and writing, determined to save this tree and others from destruction.

She stayed up there through freezing rains and winds that reached over 60 miles per hour. She stayed even though she was regularly threatened and harassed. She stayed when helicopter pilots flew less than 200 feet away from her. She stayed when the lumber company hired security guards to prevent her from receiving food and supplies. She stayed when the loggers continued to cut down ancient trees around her. She was truly committed to making the world aware of the plight of these ancient forests. Her courageous act of civil disobedience gained international media attention and became a touchstone for other environmental and social justice issues as well. That's how I heard of her.

She's pretty reclusive now, but I asked if she'd let me interview her for this book. I am grateful that she agreed to talk with me.

The first question I asked was whether she had experienced many dark nights of the soul while spending time with Luna. She said that she had many, but they didn't stop her; they helped her realize that she wanted love to be the guiding force of her life. Julia now sees her life as a sacred practice—"living love as a verb"—and is committed to leading a life of loving, joyous service. To stay on track, she regularly asks herself this question: *What would love have me think, say, and do in this moment?*

She believes each one of us needs to recognize and become deeply present to the reality that every single choice we make changes the world in some way.

"Most people actually long to live in a peaceful, loving, and caring world," she went on, "but one of the biggest challenges is to realize *all* the ways you actually make choices—through your every thought, word, and action—and how these choices either support or are harmful to this vision. Every single choice you make either leads you toward that vision or away from it. Even your choice *to do nothing* has an impact."

I share her perspective, and I make the choice to live a more conscious, caring, connected, and committed life. I imagine you do, too. You recognize the deep interdependence of all of creation and realize how your every choice shapes and affects our world and planet. As Mohandas Gandhi is quoted as saying, "Happiness is when what you think, what you say, and what you do are in harmony." That's living a life of integrity, and you can do that by making every single choice a conscious one.

The Heart Calls

You have come into this world with a unique set of desires that your heart calls you to fulfill. And inherent in each of those desires is the mechanics for its fulfillment, a complete plan that will allow for the full and continuous blossoming of love in your life. Like the blueprint of a house, it's already been created, specifically for you. I tell you this from personal experience: Life will guide you. You need only trust that it's there and be open enough and free enough of your own preconceptions to hear the call.

Discovering what lights you up can be much more difficult when your mind is filled with conditions, labels, and collected evidence of what will or won't work for you. There is a well-known Zen Buddhist story about a conversation between a learned professor of philosophy and the Zen master Nan-in. The professor was visiting the master to discover a better understanding of Zen. Nan-in welcomed him and prepared tea. He then poured tea into his visitor's cup, but continued pouring even after it was full. The professor watched the tea overflow until he no longer could restrain himself. "It is overfull," he cried. "No more will go in!"

"Exactly," said the Zen master. "Like this cup, you are full of your own opinions and speculations. You ask for teaching, but your cup is full. Before I can teach you, you'll have to empty your cup."

Before you can be filled with possibility, you too have to approach life with an "empty cup," with the beginner's mind toward others, yourself, and life. You must meet life with an open, receptive awareness, so you can notice the synchronicities and signs offered to you. On the other hand, if your mind is filled with your preferences, anxieties, fears, prejudices, assumptions, and speculations, it's almost impossible to receive the call.

Although I've offered many words throughout this book, there are really none to describe the field of love; it is beyond ideas, words, constructs, and measures. It is the most subtle, refined, and expansive aspect of you. You have to directly experience it for yourself by connecting with it on purpose, and you can use the practices you've learned in this book to do just that.

Once you become attentive to and intimate with the field of love and remove all the barriers to it expressing itself through you, all your creative endeavors—whether you're starting a company, redecorating your living room, cooking a meal for someone you love, forming a nonprofit to end hunger, protecting wildlife, making a lifestyle choice, or writing the book that's been calling to you for years—unfold with a new level of clarity, momentum, and *ease*.

Great works of art are rarely the result of strife and effort. Instead, the artist simply becomes attentive to the inner stirrings of what wants to be created and waits for inspiration to call her to action. By responding to the creative impulse calling her, the "artist" as an individual disappear. Her awareness merges with the spontaneous flow of intelligence, the source of all creativity, energy, and attention: the field of love.

When you align your personality, your way of life, and your attention with this benevolent source field, your actions become effortless and graceful, for the simple reason that you understand you are not the generator of that action, but rather the receiver of its wisdom and current.

As Lao-tzu, a philosopher and poet in ancient China, wrote in the highly regarded *Tao Te Ching*: "The Tao never does anything, yet through it all things are done."

Fall into Love

People often advise us to "Follow your dreams!" I'd hear that and ask myself, *What are my dreams?* The answer is that I couldn't possibly dream big enough because I don't know all the possibilities. Instead, I live with curiosity. I have the desire to know love, and now I follow my heart, one conscious choice at a time—and it turns out, in hindsight, to all make perfect sense.

I never imagined I'd be writing books, living in Sedona, directing the international Meditation Teacher Academy, and facilitating meditation weekends. But that is where I am today. And like the lotus that continually blossoms and opens to the sun, I am continually welcoming what is next and how I can best be used to create more love and peace on this planet.

Love lives through you as you, right now. It is propelling you toward your path to fulfillment. You, like all of us on this planet, are essential to creating more peace. You have a mission in this life, and if you don't know what it is now, it will inevitably be revealed to you at some time. Perhaps your mission is like mine, to transform the world you live in through your presence, actions, and power of love. All you have to do to discover it is to pay attention.

Notice what excites you and calls to you. Be clear about what you are committed to, and remain curious. Be open to signs and wonders, coincidence, and opportunity. Continue to connect with the field of love in meditation. Take small steps toward what calls you. Notice the responses of your body and heart as you travel. Move in the direction of joy and peace. Say yes to what arises to support you. Be courageous and trust that the field of love is living in you and through you. Above all, know that life loves you.

Love speaks to you through every possible source and seizes every opportunity to get you to merge with it. It waits for you to fully realize it, occasionally tapping you on the shoulder or catching your attention. It can call you down the street, or to the other end of the Earth.

Whatever you are called to do—whether it's to end homelessness, start a scholarship fund, teach meditation to veterans, open a children's home, take care of a loved one, or simply love yourself—I support you full-heartedly in your willingness to allow love to move through you. I support your putting love into action no matter what it looks like.

The most important relationship you can ever tend is the one you have with the source of your attention. You are an expression of this brilliant field of love. You are related to and connected to every other being, every star and particle of the universe, because of it.

You can fall into this love by remembering you *are* love, and that you are beloved by the world around you. It's easy to remember as you gaze at a spectacular sunset or spend time under the stars with the summer breeze on your skin. You fall into love when you turn your attention to that presence that is looking through your eyes, when you allow it to be called forth through you, when you generously share your unique talents and express to others the wisdom and perspective that you have embodied. Be an activist for love in action.

As you make the transformation from seeking love to being love, you realize love is never something you have to search for, become worthy of, or even earn. Love is your very nature. You only have to pay attention to it to unleash its power. And this is well within your reach. You've had the power all along.

ACKNOWLEDGMENTS

A world of love and thanks to everyone and everything, seen and unseen, whose love, support, and talents have turned the thought of this book into a reality.

I am beyond grateful to everyone who faithfully works with me at my meditation institute. Thank you, Julie Bevirt, Carol Studenka, Lisa Campbell, Christine Rolfe, Suzi von Mensenkampff, Sarah Fletcher, Zac Occhiline, Joy Nanda, Diane Dearmore, Chris Muldoon, Adrienne Pieroth, Sara Alper, Jules Green, and Pauline Lucas. You are a joy to do this work with!

And to all those who come to Sedona to meditate with me, thank you for your dedication to living a soul-centered life and for making my work matter. To the hundreds of students who have journeyed on to become meditation teachers, thank you for trusting me, being courageous, and following your heart. I truly honor you and your commitment to creating more peace on this planet.

I offer my deepest appreciation to my teachers whose presence has shined so bright and lights my way, including Ralph Waldo Emerson, Maharishi Mahesh Yogi, Deepak Chopra, Mata Amritanandamayi, Roshi Seisen Saunders, Byron Katie, Thich Nhat Hanh, Rumi, Ramana Maharshi, John O'Donohue, Teresa of Avila, and the Dalai Lama.

Many thanks go to a cadre of multitalented editors, whom I also consider friends: Danielle Dorman, Amanda Christmann Larson, Victoria Nelson, and Melissa Karolides. Thanks also to everyone at Hay House, including my editor, Nicolette Salamanca Young, for her gift of uber patience.

To my friends who stand by me, you know who you are: I am sorry, I love you, and thank you. Thank you for loving me even when you likely began to think that this book was a figment of my imagination because it took so long to finish and kept me out of touch with you.

I am in deep appreciation of my family who inspires me, especially my devoted and entertaining husband, Marty. Thank you for loving me so much, making me laugh, and keeping me company while I write. I appreciate my loving and clever dogs, Rudy and Gigi, who are always ready to hear what I write and are persistent in their attempts to get me to hike the red rocks with them. I must have really good karma.

And, finally, to my readers: thank you for choosing this book to accompany you as you become more present and powerful.

ABOUT THE AUTHOR

Sarah McLean has been meditating and teaching meditation for over two decades. She considers herself an American Transcendentalist, and her work is inspired by the Vedic, Buddhist, Christian mystic, and Taoist traditions. She teaches because she knows that connecting deeply to one's interior realm can help anyone wake up to the wonder and beauty of their life, this creation, and their interconnectedness to everything in it.

Sarah has served as the education director for the Chopra Center for Wellbeing, and directed The School for The Work of Byron Katie. She has developed and led programs for the Chopra Center, Esalen, the Sanctuary, and Mii amo Spa at Enchantment. She is a recognized leader in the field of meditation and mindfulness, and develops training programs for various multinational and Fortune 500 companies. Her work has been featured in the *New York Times*, the *Los Angeles Times*, and *Forbes Magazine*; and she has appeared on ABC, NBC, and Fox networks.

Sarah lives in Sedona, Arizona, where she founded the McLean Meditation Institute and the Meditation Teacher Academy®, a professional training program for meditation and mindfulness teachers.

Website: www.mcleanmeditation.com

Hay House Titles of Related Interest

YOU CAN HEAL YOUR LIFE, the movie, starring Louise Hay & Friends
(available as a 1-DVD program and an expanded 2-DVD set)
Watch the trailer at: www.LouiseHayMovie.com

THE SHIFT, the movie,
starring Dr. Wayne W. Dyer
(available as a 1-DVD program and an expanded 2-DVD set)
Watch the trailer at: www.DyerMovie.com

*RESILIENCE FROM THE HEART: The Power to
Thrive in Life's Extremes,* by Gregg Braden

*REVEAL: A Sacred Manual for Getting
Spiritually Naked,* by Meggan Watterson

*SECRETS OF MEDITATION: A Practical Guide
to Inner Peace and Personal Transformation,* by davidji

*THE UNIVERSE HAS YOUR BACK: Transform
Fear to Faith,* by Gabrielle Bernstein

*WHO WOULD YOU BE WITHOUT YOUR STORY?:
Dialogues with Byron Katie,* by Byron Katie

All of the above are available at your local bookstore,
or may be ordered by contacting Hay House (see next page).

We hope you enjoyed this Hay House book. If you'd like to receive our online catalog featuring additional information on Hay House books and products, or if you'd like to find out more about the Hay Foundation, please contact:

Hay House, Inc., P.O. Box 5100, Carlsbad, CA 92018-5100
(760) 431-7695 or (800) 654-5126
(760) 431-6948 (fax) or (800) 650-5115 (fax)
www.hayhouse.com® • www.hayfoundation.org

Published and distributed in Australia by:
Hay House Australia Pty. Ltd., 18/36 Ralph St., Alexandria NSW 2015
Phone: 612-9669-4299 • *Fax:* 612-9669-4144 • www.hayhouse.com.au

Published and distributed in the United Kingdom by:
Hay House UK, Ltd., Astley House, 33 Notting Hill Gate, London W11 3JQ
Phone: 44-20-3675-2450 • *Fax:* 44-20-3675-2451 • www.hayhouse.co.uk

Published and distributed in the Republic of South Africa by:
Hay House SA (Pty), Ltd., P.O. Box 990, Witkoppen 2068
info@hayhouse.co.za • www.hayhouse.co.za

Published in India by: Hay House Publishers India,
Muskaan Complex, Plot No. 3, B-2, Vasant Kunj, New Delhi 110 070
Phone: 91-11-4176-1620 • *Fax:* 91-11-4176-1630 • www.hayhouse.co.in

Distributed in Canada by: Raincoast Books,
2440 Viking Way, Richmond, B.C. V6V 1N2
Phone: 1-800-663-5714 • *Fax:* 1-800-565-3770 • www.raincoast.com

Take Your Soul on a Vacation

Visit www.HealYourLife.com® to regroup, recharge,
and reconnect with your own magnificence.
Featuring blogs, mind-body-spirit news, and
life-changing wisdom from Louise Hay and friends.

Visit www.HealYourLife.com today!